Cut Your Tax In Half

**START YOUR OWN
TAX REDUCTION
PLANNING PROCESS**
visit
http://www.CutYourTaxInHalf.com

Cut Your Tax In Half

WEALTH BUILDING BY
TAX PLANNING

● ● ●

Harak Gala, CPA

Copyright © 2017 Etax Corporation, Columbia, Maryland, USA

ISBN-13: 9781540716958
ISBN-10: 1540716953

All rights reserved. No part of this book may be reproduced or transmitted in any form or by any means without the prior written permission of the author, except in the case of brief quotations embodied in critical reviews and certain other noncommercial uses permitted by copyright law.

Disclaimers and Disclosures

• • •

THE INFORMATION AND STRATEGIES PROVIDED in this book are for general purposes only and may not apply to your particular situation. Tax laws are complex, and the suggestions given in this book are not for do-it-yourselfers. The strategies contained in this book may not be suitable for your situation and, in fact, may work against your goals and needs. Before implementing any suggestions from this book, you must consult your own professional tax or financial adviser. In some cases, a team of advisers may be warranted. While we have used our best efforts to complete the book, neither the author nor his affiliates are responsible for any errors, omissions, incompleteness, or inaccuracy in the contents of this book. The author and his affiliates do not make any representation or warranties with respect to the contents of this book and specifically disclaim any warranties of merchantability or fitness for any particular purpose. The author and his affiliates shall not be liable for any damages directly or indirectly.

Tax planning, financial planning, and wealth strategies are only to alert you about some possibilities but are not for implementing without consulting your own professional tax and financial advisers. The hypothetical illustrations given in this book are for information purposes only and should not be a representation of any particular investment. Past performance is not a guarantee for future results. Before investing, investors should carefully consider the investment objectives, risks, charges, expenses, underlying investment options, and current prospectuses. Funds withdrawn from traditional retirement accounts are subject to ordinary income tax when distributed and will be subject to 10 percent penalty tax if withdrawn before age fifty-nine and a half.

Annuities are long-term investments designed for retirement. Guarantees provided by annuities are backed by claim-paying ability of that insurance company only. Earnings are subject to ordinary income tax when distributed and will be subject to 10 percent penalty tax if withdrawn before age fifty-nine and a half. The primary purpose of life insurance is to provide a death benefit and is only one component of an overall financial strategy. Indexed universal insurance policies also offer the opportunity for cash-value accumulation. Loans/withdrawals may be taken against available cash value for any purpose, including supplemental retirement income.

To the extent that this material concerns tax matters, it is not intended or written to be used, and cannot be used, by a taxpayer for the purpose of avoiding penalties that may be imposed by law. Each taxpayer should seek independent advice from a tax professional based on his or her individual circumstances.

These materials are provided for general information and educational purposes based on publicly available information from sources believed to be reliable—we cannot assure the accuracy or completeness of these materials. The information in these materials may change at any time and without notice.

The tax scenarios given in this book are inspired by real-life cases, but the client names are not real. Even the amounts given in the tax returns are changed to keep the privacy of our clients.

We realize that readers of this book may have limited tax knowledge and may not thoroughly understand all the tax strategies given in this book. But again, the purpose of this book is not to make you an expert in taxes. The purpose is to emphasize the importance of tax planning.

To my mother, Laxmi

Mother, what I am today is because of you. You sacrificed many important things in your life to shape my career and make my future brighter. And when I was nearly ready to give part of it back to you, you were gone forever...

No, Mother, you are not gone. You are still here with me in my heart, guiding me and showing me the light every step of the way, as I continue my journey in this mysterious world.

Acknowledgements

● ● ●

First, thanks to my wife Nalini for having the patience with me for having taking yet another challenge which decreases the amount of time I can spend with her.

I want to thank many of my clients for sharing my happiness and giving me encouragement to write this book. I also want to acknowledge valuable input from Suchita Gala, Purvi Gala, and Rachel Milne in completing this book.

Contents

Disclaimers and Disclosures · v
Acknowledgements · ix
Introduction · xiii

Chapter 1 Software Developers · 1
Chapter 2 Alternate Minimum Tax · 20
Chapter 3 Business Entity · 34
Chapter 4 Change of Profession · 43
Chapter 5 Social-Security Taxes · 56
Chapter 6 Small-Business Retirement Plans · · · · · · · · · · · · · · · · · 63
Chapter 7 Tax-Free Retirement Using IRS Notice 2014-54· · · · · · · · · 73
Chapter 8 Tax-Free Retirement Using IRS Code Sections 7702 & 72(e) · · 77
Chapter 9 Working as a Team · 82

Author's Note · 87

Introduction

• • •

THE YEAR WAS 1984, AND I was working as an engineer in Maryland for a multinational manufacturing company. One day I stepped out of my office for lunch, and as I passed a nearby steel-workers union building, I saw a group of people standing still. Each of them wore a sign around his or her neck that stated, "I am paying more income tax than GE." It piqued my curiosity. How could a normal person be paying more income tax than a huge corporation such as General Electric? Initially, I thought this must be some kind of joke, but those demonstrators looked very serious.

I tried to forget the incident, but it kept banging around in the back of my mind. I just couldn't let it go, so I decided to do some research. In those days, information was not as readily available as it is today—back then Google was just a number most people had never heard of!—so I headed off to the library. After going through a few old newspapers, I found that, in fact, General Electric had not paid *any* income tax in the previous few years, in spite of making huge profits. On further research, I found that GE was not the only company skipping out on taxes—many highly profitable companies were paying *zero* income tax!

Now I was really curious. I went home and looked at a copy of my own tax return. What was *I* doing wrong? How could I be paying so much in taxes while others got away with paying little to nothing at all? After all, I was a logical thinker and very strong with numbers. I had both engineering and MBA degrees. I double-checked my tax calculations and went through the IRS instruction book again. There were no mistakes. I even acquired as many tax books as I could. While those books did a good job explaining how to prepare my tax return, none had the answers I was seeking: how to lower my taxes. My research continued. I slowly started to understand the different kinds of tax strategies being used by many wealthy individuals and big corporations.

Meanwhile, at work, my company's US branch kept growing. In a twist of fate, I became more involved with our corporate finances and took on the responsibility of preparing our corporate tax returns. Shortly thereafter, I became immersed in tax strategies and received a promotion to treasurer for the US branch. At this point, I saw the writing on the wall. I realized that this kind of work was exciting to me. It did not feel like a work at all. So I decided to become a certified public accountant (CPA).

A few years passed. In 1993, as a relatively new CPA, I was ready to start my own part-time tax business with the skills and strategies I had learned. As my tax business was only seasonal and maintaining an office year-round was not economically feasible, I started my business from the basement of my own home.

Starting a new business is never easy. I remember setting up my card table in a local Parcel Plus, with the owner's permission, and reaching out to the customers coming into the store. In the first year, I managed to get a few clients. Oddly enough, I helped those clients not only in preparing their taxes but also in analyzing their tax returns for future tax-planning opportunities. Additionally, I also filed amended tax returns for previous years to get many of my clients additional refunds! Those clients liked my approach and were so happy that they began to refer others to me. As the referrals kept coming, my business quadrupled the very next year. Most of my clients had never encountered this kind of pleasant tax-preparation experience before. But as an analytical, logical person, I didn't know any other way of preparing taxes; I only did what I thought was right.

One day, as I prepared taxes for a new client, she was pleased with the results but mentioned that, the previous year, she had owed a large sum of money after filing. I was surprised to hear this, because she had a relatively simple return. She mentioned that, after her husband's death, she had sold some stocks he'd owned. Her tax preparer had made her pay those taxes because of the capital gain on those stocks. After looking at her previous year's tax return, however, I asked her several questions. Based on the answers she gave, I ended up filing an amended return for her. And when she got a five-figure refund from the IRS for the previous year, she came back to me, hugged me, and started crying. She really needed that money and could not stop crying for a few minutes. It gave me great joy to see that she'd recovered the money that rightfully belonged to her. This, and many other stories like it, strengthened my determination to help people. This wasn't work anymore—I had a new purpose.

As I prepared tax returns for my clients, I also looked at their investment statements from a tax-efficiency point of view. Whenever I saw the possibility of reducing their taxes, I told them to talk to their brokers or financial advisers about it. The response was mixed. I was especially worried about the smaller investors, who I felt were not getting the service they deserved. Some of my clients even asked me to handle their investments, but I told them I was not licensed to do so. Many of my clients suggested I get the required licenses. When I thought about the idea, I came to the conclusion that, in order to best serve my clients, I either needed to create an ongoing relationship with a financial adviser or to seek licensure myself. Ultimately, I decided to become a financial adviser.

I studied all aspects of financial planning, such as investments, retirement-income allocation, estate planning, legacy planning, and protection planning. I also got my FINRA, SEC, and insurance licenses. I regularly took part in many conferences throughout the country to keep myself updated on the latest available investment opportunities. As I began to learn more, I was able to offer even better services to my tax clients, who benefited tremendously. Soon I outgrew my basement and moved to an office building.

Over the years, the one key fact I've learned through my experience is this: tax preparation and tax planning are two completely different things. Most people meet their CPAs only once between February and April to do the work of tax preparation and filing. All their tax documents are already in black and white, and neither the clients nor their CPAs have much control on the final outcome at that point. It is too late for tax planning.

The *real* time for tax planning is between May and December. Over time, the tax system has become so complex that most of us really don't understand it; however, the tax code provides many tax-planning opportunities for those who are proactive. The money you pay in taxes is gone forever, but the money you *save* in taxes makes you even *more* money during your lifetime. With proper planning, it is easier to save a lot of money owed in taxes than to take huge risks by chasing high returns on speculative investments. In fact, tax planning and financial planning are two sides of the same coin, and the best planning is done when your CPA and your financial adviser sit in the same room. *If they don't talk to each other, you're the one who suffers!*

This book contains examples of how, with proper planning, you can reduce your taxes substantially. But these tax-planning techniques are not do-it-yourself projects—the IRS has a lot of requirements and restrictions for implementing these strategies, so you must execute them with professional help. That being said, if you take the time to properly consider and plan for your tax and financial situation early, you will reap the rewards when you file your returns.

Below are summaries for the chapters of this book. Each chapter illustrates different types of tax-planning strategies, followed by copies of tax returns before and after implementation of those strategies.

Chapter 1 shows the case of software engineers Sam and Sonya. Their tax return before any planning showed a tax liability of $80,077. Based upon their income, they were not receiving any child tax credit, even though they had three children under seventeen. They were also being subjected to Alternative Minimum Tax (AMT), additional Medicare taxes, and net-investment taxes. By simply implementing a few tax-planning strategies, they were able to get the child tax credit, while AMT, additional Medicare taxes, and net-investment taxes either decreased or disappeared completely! These changes reduced their federal tax liability from $80,077 to $40,248 and their state liability from $22,794 to $11,712—and they can continue to use this strategy year after year. The chapter further describes the concept of backdoor Roth IRAs for people who are not eligible to contribute to their Roth IRAs.

Chapter 2 tells the story of Sean the salesman. Sean was a salaried employee who received a W-2 from his employer at the end of the year. His salary was determined simply by the amount of sales he generated. The type of W-2 he was getting from his employer was causing him to pay $15,903 as Alternative Minimum Tax (AMT). With some helpful tax planning, Sean learned he simply had to ask his employer to issue his W-2 in a different way. The employer had nothing to lose and agreed, and this simple change reduced Sean's federal tax liability from $41,414 to $20,638. His AMT completely disappeared too. Sean still earned the same income, but he had an additional $20,976 in his pocket—thanks to proper tax planning.

Chapter 3 describes the situation of Ray, a maintenance worker who lived with his wife, Rhonda, and their two children. It was very hard for Ray to support his family on his salary as a maintenance worker, so he decided to get into the business of managing maintenance contracts. He quit his job and formed a sole-member limited-liability company (LLC). His hard work, experience, and good relations with some of his contacts paid off, and Ray made very good money within the first year of his business. Ray and Rhonda were happy, but their happiness was short-lived. In the past, they'd never paid any federal tax, because they'd been eligible for day-care credit, child tax credit, and college credit. This year their regular tax liability was negligible because of all those credits; however, they owed $12,151 in self-employment tax. Please read the chapter to find out how they were able to reduce their self-employment tax liability from $12,151 to $6,579.

Chapter 4 illustrates the situation of a young couple, Mark and Mary. Mark was a construction manager, while his wife, Mary, was involved in network marketing of door-to-door sales. They also had two rental properties, which they had bought in 2007. The market values of those properties went down considerably during the 2008 market downturn. Mark and Mary were losing a considerable amount on those rental properties, and to their frustration, they could not deduct those losses in their tax return—according to the IRS, Mark was making too much money. With proper planning, they were able to reduce their tax liability from $24,589 to $12,886 with no change in their income or expenses.

Chapter 5 describes the tax situation of a retired couple, Ronald and Jennifer. With proper tax planning and reallocation of some of their assets, we were able to reduce their tax liability from $5,014 to zero. This chapter gives further details on several social-security planning strategies that can help drastically increase the social-security income of many retired or soon-to-be retired couples over their lifetime.

Chapter 6 explains several retirement-plan strategies for self-employed professionals. Most of us are familiar with IRAs, 401(k)s, 403(b)s, and 457s—these are defined-contribution plans; however, their contribution limits are low, and many professionals are looking to make much larger contributions. This chapter describes several *other* plans, such as traditional defined-benefit (DB) plans, 419(e) plans, and cash-balance plans. With all these plans, the tax deduction could be $100,000 or more every year. In many such cases, professionals do not have to come up with any new money or change their asset allocation. Simply by changing the titles of some of his or her investments, an investor can establish a DB plan. The chapter illustrates this point with the case of John and Jessica, who were both doctors. Please read the chapter to find out how they reduced their taxes by $188,000 simply by titling some of their investments differently and without changing their asset-allocation plan. This chapter further describes Roth conversion strategies. With so many new types of taxes—such as the Alternate Minimum Tax, Net-Investment Income Tax, and new Medicare taxes—it has become more important than ever to implement planning strategies to avoid such taxes completely or partially.

Chapter 7 addresses professionals who are not self-employed. As shown in the previous chapter, there are big tax breaks available for high-income professionals who own their own businesses…but what about high-income salaried professionals who work for others? Many of them also end up paying other taxes, such as AMT, in addition to their regular federal and state taxes. Many of them have a marginal tax bracket of more than 50 percent. If this fits your situation, then you are probably already contributing to your 401(k), 403(b), or 457 plans. The maximum annual contribution limit on such plans is $18,000 ($24,000 for age fifty or above). Many of you contribute to Roth versions of such plans, but the total limit on both the deductible and Roth is still $18,000 ($24,000 if you're fifty or older). What if you want to contribute the maximum amount in a deductible 401(k) to reduce your taxes and also some additional amount for creating tax-free retirement income? Until now this was not possible, but a notice from the IRS in September 2014 changed everything. Depending on your company plan, now you can contribute the maximum amount to your deductible 401(k) and also an additional amount in a nondeductible 401(k) subject to some limitations. (You can convert this nondeductible 401(k) amount into a Roth IRA later without paying any taxes, if you meet certain requirements.)

Chapter 8 talks about how to create tax-free retirement income using IRS code sections 7702 and section 72(e) of the life-insurance contract with the life-insurance company. The primary purpose of life insurance is death benefits, but if structured properly, it can also be used to create tax-free retirement income in terms of policy loans. This strategy has been around for a long time, but most people are not aware of it. Many older people learn about it too late, losing the opportunity they would have had if only they'd known about it twenty or thirty years earlier. It may be too late for them to take advantage of this strategy, but what about their children or even grandchildren? An early start with tax planning can help create long-term tax benefits.

Chapter 9 is the final chapter of the book, but by no means is it the end of the tax-planning strategies. In fact, this is the beginning of implementing tax- and financial-planning strategies based on your unique situation. The purpose of this book is not to describe all the possible tax-savings strategies available—*that* could not be contained in a book of this size. The purpose of this book is to make you think outside the box. Your CPA can help, and your financial adviser can help, but it is up to you to take the first step. Your CPA wants to do the best job possible, but he or she cannot help you with all your needs. Similarly, your financial adviser wants to take care of you, but his or her tax knowledge is very limited. Tax planning and financial planning go hand in hand, and if they don't move together, you'll be the one who suffers.

If the super-rich can reduce their taxes in spite of earning much more than you, then why can't you? It takes determination and preplanning.

The tax code is complex, and one mistake could not only cost you dearly now but also could have future implications. As I mentioned earlier, the strategies described in this book are not so you can avoid professionals and do it all yourself; rather, this book is to motivate you to take action and ask the right kinds of questions of your tax and financial professionals. The purpose of this book is to inspire you to make your CPA and financial planner work together in your best interest.

Many people take a very high risk just to make a few extra percentage of return on their investments, yet they miss big opportunities to save 30, 40, or even 50 percent on the amount of taxes they are paying. With a long-term tax-planning strategy, you can build massive wealth without any undue risk. I sincerely hope the case studies, examples, and strategies in this book help you toward a new way of thinking about taxes. The more you hate taxes, the more you will love this book. Let's get started!

CHAPTER 1

Software Developers

• • •

SAM AND SONYA ARE BOTH software engineers. Sonya works for a large corporation. Sam used to work for another software company, but about three years ago, he quit his nine-to-five job and started taking independent contracts to design and develop software models for several different software developers. Initially, business was slow, but it started growing steadily.

In the past, Sam and Sonya received a good annual refund due to the child tax credit they got because of their three young children, who were ages eight, twelve, and fourteen. Every year, Sam and Sonya looked forward to the tax season in anticipation of a large refund. But things changed once Sam's business started growing. In spite of paying their estimated taxes, they owed a sizable amount after filing last year, and Sam started to think starting his own business was not a good idea after all—what good was it to make more money, if they couldn't keep it? He *almost* decided to go back to his nine-to-five job. At that point, one of his friends suggested Sam come see me. Sam was not convinced. He started believing that once you make more money, you have to pay taxes at a much higher rate. After all, he had known his tax professional for many years, and seeing somebody else was not going to change the tax law.

Sonya, however, was of a different school of thought: she believed in the value of a second opinion. She knew that many rich people pay taxes at much lower effective tax rates. And, after all, the same tax law applies to every US taxpayer. She convinced Sam to make an appointment with our company. As usual, our appointment taker asked them to bring their tax returns for the last three years and the latest statements of their investments, including their old and current 401(k) statements.

When they came to our office, I looked at their tax return. (This document is figure 1-1.) Their accountant had prepared the return accurately, with all business income and expenses reported correctly. Their federal tax liability was $80,077, and their state-tax liability was $22,794. Their federal tax liability included the following:

- Regular income tax (Form 1040: page 2, line 44)
- Alternate Minimum Tax (Form 1040: page 2, line 45)
- Self-employment tax (Form 1040: page 2, line 57)
- Additional Medicare Tax (Form 1040: page 2, line 62a)
- Net Investment Income Tax (Form 1040: page 2, line 62b)

Author: Sam and Sonya, congratulations! You made a lot more money last year than you did in previous years.

Sonya: Yes, but it was not that easy. Sam really worked very hard, and we had to make many sacrifices as a family.

Sam: And now they are punishing us for working hard. We don't mind paying our fair share, but do we have to pay so many different types of taxes? Take, for example, line 45, called Alternate Minimum Tax—why are we paying these additional taxes?

Author: Let's look at Form 6251 for Alternate Minimum Tax (AMT) calculations. You are paying AMT because you pay too much in state taxes.

Sonya: What? The federal government is punishing us for paying too much in state taxes? Let's reduce our tax payments to the state!

Author: You can't do that. If you don't pay the required taxes, the state will penalize you.

Sonya: And if we do, the federal government will punish us!

Author: The state-tax payments are deductible for calculating federal tax liability. When you have too many deductions like that, the IRS wants you to calculate your taxes in two different ways. If your tax calculations using the AMT way are higher than they are the regular way, you pay the difference as AMT. Some people consider it a "stealth" tax.

Sam: What is this line 62: Taxes from Form 8959 and Form 8960? Why are we paying these additional taxes?

Author: Form 8959 is a broad category for additional taxes. In your case, once your income exceeds certain limits, you need to pay additional Medicare taxes. Form 8960 is for Net Investment Income Tax. You had some capital gains on your financial statement, which triggers Net Investment Income Tax. These taxes are also considered "stealth" taxes by many.

Sam: So you can't change anything for us—I knew it. I told Sonya we're wasting our time seeking a second opinion.

Author: I can't reduce your taxes for last year...but if you don't change anything now, assuming similar income next year, you'll pay similar taxes.

Sam: Yes, but what can we do except go back to a nine-to-five job? I definitely don't want to do anything illegal. I'm sorry to take up your time. We should be leaving now.

Author: Wait a minute. I'm not done. Can I ask you a few questions?

Sonya: Sure.

Author: Sam, do your children help you in your business?

Sam: Yes, both of our older children help me with paper filing, data entry, et cetera.

Author: Do you pay them?

Sam: No.

Author: Why not?

Sam: We are spending enough on our children. Isn't it their duty to help me in my business?

Author: I know you are spending a lot on your children, and you will be spending even more when they're ready to go to college. I'm trying to help you reduce your taxes and at the same time create a tax-free college fund for them. As your dependents, they don't pay any tax for the first $6,300 of income they earn; after that, they pay only 10 percent in federal taxes for the approximate income of another $9,200. Also, when you hire your children under eighteen in your own unincorporated business, you do not need to deduct any Social-Security or Medicare taxes, and they do not have to pay any self-employment taxes either. Assuming you pay

$6,300 per year to each of your two older children from your business, they do not have to pay any income tax, and you can deduct $12,600 from your business income. This reduces your regular income tax, Alternate Minimum Tax, self-employment tax, additional Medicare tax, and state income tax.

Sonya: Wow!

Sam: We never thought of it that way.

Author: It gets better. Each of your children can open his or her Roth IRA and invest $5,500 from that $6,300. We will talk about this in our next meeting, but for now, let's talk about your own taxes further. Sam, you are eligible to establish a retirement plan for yourself from your business. There are many different types of plans available, but in your situation, I recommend a traditional defined-benefit (DB) plan combined with a 401(k) plan. Based on your age and income, you can invest $92,000 as employer contribution and $18,000 as employee contribution. So you can contribute a total of $110,000 a year and deduct the whole amount from your taxes.

Sam: But I do not have an extra $110,000 in cash to put in this plan. Can I use some of my nonqualified investments to open such a plan?

Author: We will talk about your investments in the next meeting. Before we make any changes to your investments, we do have to run a suitability analysis. Also, we have to make sure that any changes we make are in your best interest. We will talk about all that in our next meeting. Today, we will concentrate only on identifying potential tax-saving opportunities. Let me run some numbers quickly and see how your tax return could look like if we do implement these strategies.

I prepared another tax return, as shown in figure 1-2. I wanted Sonya and Sam to see how their liabilities and credits might change if they decided to move forward with my recommendations.

Author: Please look at this tax return, and you'll see a few major changes:

1. Alternate Minimum Tax completely goes away.
2. Net Investment Tax completely goes away.

3. Additional Medicare tax gets reduced.
4. Your total federal tax liability reduces from $80,077 to $40,248.
5. Your state-tax liability reduces from $22,794 to $11,712.

Your total tax liability for both federal and state together reduces from $102,871 to $50,950, which means you would see a tax savings of $50,921.

Sam: Wow! But don't we have to pay taxes when we take that money out from the retirement plans?

Author: Yes, you do. The money you pay in taxes is gone forever and never gets a chance to grow. With tax-deferred retirement plans, 100 percent of your investments have a potential to grow. At some point, either when you close these plans or when you stop working, we will have an opportunity to convert the funds from these plans into a traditional IRA first and ultimately into a Roth IRA. Our strategy will be to convert most of these funds, if not all of them, to Roth over many years in the most tax-efficient way before you reach seventy years of age; this could make your retirement after seventy mostly tax-free forever. We will be converting your taxable assets into tax-free assets in two steps. The first step will be to convert taxable money into tax-deferred money, and the second step will be to convert tax-deferred money into tax-free money. The money you would have been paying in taxes would have been gone forever, but now that money will also have a chance to grow. Also, you will not be paying dreaded taxes such as AMT and Net Investment Income Taxes.

Sam: Sounds like a good idea. When can we get started?

Author: We will need the services of a third-party administrator (TPA), and it will cost you about $2,500 per year. Also, this is not just a one-year plan; once you start, you will have to continue it for many years and contribute similar amounts every year.

Sam: If we can save $51,000, we can afford to pay $2,500 to the TPA. I have no doubt about the continuity of the business—I feel confident I'll make more money in future years.

Sonya: Sounds good. Speaking of Roth IRAs, you mentioned something about Roth IRAs for our children earlier.

Author: Sure. You will be giving $6,300 salary to each of your two older children every year for many years. If they continue to put $5,500 out of that $6,300 in their Roth IRAs year after year for all those years, they could potentially have sizable amounts to meet their college expenses. They could take out their original investment in the Roth IRA after five years without paying any taxes or penalties. And if your children get scholarships and don't need to use the money for education, they can use it for their own retirement. And there's more! Once your children see their tax-free accounts growing, they will form a habit to keep contributing even after they start working independently somewhere else. You can't put a price tag on teaching your children this positive behavior at a very young age.

Sam: They can do that for a few years, but once they grow up and start making big money, they won't be eligible for Roth IRA contributions. Am I correct?

Author: That is true, but there is a work-around to that situation. Let me explain: Even after they start making big bucks, they will be able to contribute in a nondeductible IRA. Since they don't have any traditional IRA accounts, they can immediately convert that nondeductible IRA into a Roth IRA without paying any taxes. They can continue to do so irrespective of how much money they will be making.

Sonya: Is it legal?

Author: Per the IRS code, there's nothing illegal about it. It can be done legally.

Sonya: That's great. Can we get everything started now?

Author: No. Today we talked about potential tax-savings strategies. Before we implement any of these strategies, I have to evaluate them from a financial-planning point of view. I have to make sure that any changes we make in your investments are suitable, based on your needs, goals, and risk tolerance. Whatever changes we make, if any, must be in your best interest.

Sam: I didn't believe in a second opinion earlier, but now, I'm a strong believer. During our discussion, we talked about Alternate Minimum Tax. My friend Sean was telling me he pays quite a bit of Alternate Minimum

Tax. He also doesn't believe too much in second opinions, but I think I can convince him to see you. Can you see him?

Author: Certainly.

Sam: Great. I'll let him know and also tell him what a wonderful experience we had in this meeting.

Sonya: We can't wait until our next meeting. Thank you very much.

Author: Thank you for your visit. See you soon.

Form 1040 — U.S. Individual Income Tax Return (2015)

Department of the Treasury — Internal Revenue Service — OMB No. 1545-0074

For the year Jan. 1–Dec. 31, 2015, or other tax year beginning ____, 2015, ending ____, 20__

Your first name and initial: Sam **Last name:** Taxpayer **Your social security number:** 400-01-1001

If a joint return, spouse's first name and initial: Sonya **Last name:** Taxpayer **Spouse's social security number:** 400-01-2001

Home address (number and street): 123 Main Street

City, town or post office, state, and ZIP code: COLUMBIA MD 21045-

Filing Status
2. [X] Married filing jointly (even if only one had income)

Exemptions
- 6a [X] Yourself
- 6b [X] Spouse
- 6c Dependents:

(1) First name Last name	(2) Dependent's social security number	(3) Relationship to you	(4) ✓ if qualifying child for child tax credit
Jay Taxpayer	400-01-3001	SON	[X]
Jessica Taxpayer	400-01-4001	DAUGHTER	[X]
Jim Taxpayer	400-00-5001	SON	[X]

Boxes checked on 6a and 6b: **2**
No. of children on 6c who lived with you: **3**

Income

7	Wages, salaries, tips, etc. Attach Form(s) W-2	100,000.
8a	Taxable interest. Attach Schedule B if required	1,000.
8b	Tax-exempt interest. Do not include on line 8a	
9a	Ordinary dividends. Attach Schedule B if required	3,400.
9b	Qualified dividends	2,000.
12	Business income or (loss). Attach Schedule C or C-EZ	182,000.
13	Capital gain or (loss). Attach Schedule D if required. If not required, check here [X]	7,000.
22	Combine the amounts in the far right column for lines 7 through 21. This is your **total income**	293,400.

Adjusted Gross Income

Line	Description	Amount
27	Deductible part of self-employment tax. Attach Schedule SE	9,784.
36	Add lines 23 through 35	9,784.
37	Subtract line 36 from line 22. This is your **adjusted gross income**	283,616.

For Disclosure, Privacy Act, and Paperwork Reduction Act Notice, see separate instructions.

Form **1040** (2015)

Figure 1-1 Page 1

Cut Your Tax In Half

Figure 1-1 Page 2

MARYLAND FORM 502 RESIDENT INCOME TAX RETURN 2015

OR FISCAL YEAR BEGINNING _____ 2015, ENDING _____

400011001 — Social Security Number
400012001 — Spouse's Social Security Number

Sam — Your First Name
Taxpayer — Your Last Name

Sonya — Spouse's First Name
Taxpayer — Spouse's Last Name

123 Main Street — Current Mailing Address

COLUMBIA, MD 21045

Maryland County: **HW**

FILING STATUS (Check one box):
3. ☒ Married filing joint return or spouse had no income

EXEMPTIONS
- A. ☒ Yourself ☒ Spouse — Enter number checked: 2
- D. Total Exemptions: 3 — Total Amount: D.

INCOME
1. Adjusted gross income from your federal return 1. 283616
   - 1a. Wages, salaries and/or tips: 100000
   - 1c. Capital Gain or (loss): 7000
1e. ☒ Check here if the amount of your investment income is more than $11,000

ADDITIONS TO INCOME
7. Total federal adjusted gross income and Maryland additions (Add lines 1 and 6): 283616

COM/RAD-009

Figure 1-1 Page 3

Cut Your Tax In Half

Figure 1-1 Page 4

11

Harak Gala, CPA

Figure 1-1 Page 5

Cut Your Tax In Half

Figure 1-2 Page 1

Figure 1-2 Page 2

Cut Your Tax In Half

Figure 1-2 Page 3

Harak Gala, CPA

MARYLAND FORM **502**	RESIDENT INCOME	2015 Page 2

NAME: Sam & Sonya Taxpayer   SSN: 400021001

SUBTRACTIONS FROM INCOME
See Instruction 13

Line	Description	Amount
8	Taxable refunds, credits or offsets of state and local income taxes included in line 1	
9	Child and dependent care expenses	
10	Pension exclusion from worksheet in Instruction 13	
11	Taxable Social Security and RR benefits (Tier I, II and supplemental) included in line 1	
12	Income received during period of nonresidence (See Instruction 26)	
13	Subtractions from attached Form 502SU	
14	Two-income subtraction from worksheet in Instruction 13	1200
15	Total subtractions from Maryland income (Add lines 8 through 14)	1200
16	Maryland adjusted gross income (Subtract line 15 from line 7)	159984

DEDUCTION METHOD
See Instruction 16

All taxpayers must select one method and check the appropriate box.
☒ STANDARD DEDUCTION METHOD (Enter amount on line 17)
☐ ITEMIZED DEDUCTION METHOD (Complete lines 17a and 17b)

17a	Total federal itemized deductions (from line 29, federal Schedule A)	18500
17b	State and local income taxes (See Instruction 14)	18500
	Subtract line 17b from line 17a and enter amount on line 17	
17	Deduction amount (Part-year residents see Instruction 26 l and m)	4000
18	Net income (Subtract line 17 from line 16)	155984
19	Exemption amount from Exemptions area (See Instruction 10)	8000
20	Taxable net income (Subtract line 19 from line 18)	147984

MARYLAND TAX COMPUTATION

Line	Description	Amount
21	Maryland tax (from Tax Table or Computation Worksheet Schedules I or II)	6977
22	Earned income credit (% of federal earned income credit. See Instruction 18)	
23	Poverty level credit (See Instruction 18)	
24	Other income tax credits for individuals from Part J, line 10 of Form 502CR (Attach Form 502CR)	
25	Business tax credits... You must file this form electronically to claim business tax credits on Form 500CR	
26	Total credits (Add lines 22 through 25)	
27	Maryland tax after credits (Subtract line 26 from line 21) If less than 0, enter 0	6977

LOCAL TAX COMPUTATION

Line	Description	Amount
28	Local tax (See Instruction 19 for tax rates and worksheet) Multiply line 20 by your local tax rate 0.320 or use the Local Tax Worksheet	4735
29	Local earned income credit (from Local Earned Income Credit Worksheet in Instruction 19)	
30	Local poverty level credit (from Local Poverty Level Credit Worksheet in Instruction 19)	
31	Local tax credit from Part K, line 1 of Form 502CR (Attach Form 502CR)	
32	Total credits (Add lines 29 through 31)	
33	Local tax after credits (Subtract line 32 from line 28) If less than 0, enter 0	4735
34	Total Maryland and local tax (Add lines 27 and 33)	11712
35	Contribution to Chesapeake Bay and Endangered Species Fund (See Instruction 20)	
36	Contribution to Developmental Disabilities Services and Support Fund (See Instruction 20)	
37	Contribution to Maryland Cancer Fund (See Instruction 20)	
38	Contribution to Fair Campaign Financing Fund (See Instruction 20)	
39	**Total Maryland income tax, local income tax and contributions** (Add lines 34 through 38)	11712
40	Total Maryland and local tax withheld (Enter total from your W-2 and 1099 forms if MD tax is withheld and attach)	5000
41	2015 estimated tax payments, amount applied from 2014 return, payment made with an extension request, and Form MW506NRS	18000
42	Refundable earned income credit (from worksheet in Instruction 21)	
43	Refundable income tax credits from Part L, line 6 of Form 502CR (Attach Form 502CR. See Instruction 21)	
44	Total payments and credits (Add lines 40 through 43)	23000

Figure 1-2 Page 4

Cut Your Tax In Half

MARYLAND FORM **502**	RESIDENT INCOME TAX RETURN		2015 Page 3

NAME Sam & Sonya Taxpayer   SSN 400021001

REFUND	45. Balance due (If line 39 is more than line 44, subtract line 44 from line 39 See Instruction 22.)	►45	
	46. Overpayment (If line 39 is less than line 44, subtract line 39 from line 44.)	►46	11288
	47. Amount of overpayment TO BE APPLIED TO 2016 ESTIMATED TAX ►47		
	48. Amount of overpayment TO BE REFUNDED TO YOU (Subtract line 47 from line 46.) See line 51.	REFUND ►48	11288
	49. Interest charges from Form 502UP _____ or for late filing (See Instruction 22.) Total	►49	
AMOUNT DUE	50. TOTAL AMOUNT DUE (Add lines 45 and 49.) IF $1 OR MORE, PAY IN FULL WITH THIS RETURN	50	

DIRECT DEPOSIT OF REFUND (See Instruction 22.) Be sure the account information is correct. **For Splitting Direct Deposit, see Form 588.** If this refund will go to an account outside of the United States, then to comply with banking rules, place a "Y" in this box ► ☐ and see Instruction 22. For the direct deposit option, complete the following information clearly and legibly.

51a. Type of account: ► ☐ Checking   ☐ Savings

51b. Routing Number (9-digits) ►   51c. Account Number

►
Daytime telephone no.   Home telephone no.   CODE NUMBERS (3 digits per line)

Check here ☐ if you authorize your preparer to discuss this return with us. Check here ► ☐
if you authorize your paid preparer not to file electronically. Check here ☐ if you agree to
receive your 1099G Income Tax Refund statement electronically. (See Instruction 24.)

Make checks payable to and mail to:
Comptroller of Maryland
Revenue Administration Division
110 Carroll Street
Annapolis, Maryland 21411-0001

Under penalties of perjury, I declare that I have examined this return, including accompanying schedules and statements and to the best of my knowledge and belief it is true, correct and complete. If prepared by a person other than taxpayer, the declaration is based on all information of which the preparer has any knowledge.

It is recommended that you include your Social Security Number on check.

Your signature   Date

Spouse's signature   Date

Harak Gala CPA
Signature of preparer other than taxpayer

727 Thornwood Dr
Street address of preparer

ODENTON MD 21113
City, State, ZIP

3019123450
Telephone number of preparer

P01201436
Preparer's PTIN (required by law)

COM/RAD-009

Figure 1-2 Page 5

Notes

Notes

CHAPTER 2

Alternate Minimum Tax

• • •

SEAN IS A SALESMAN, ALWAYS on the road. His salary is based strictly on commission. The more he drives, the more money he makes. Sean's employer does not reimburse his business-related expenses, so he keeps good records of his own expenses for tax purposes. His wife, Sally, does not work. They have two children. They brought their tax returns and investment statements for our appointment.

I looked at their latest return, which appears in figure 2-1.

Author: Sean and Sally, you are making pretty good money for your age. Congratulations!

Sean: Yes, but it comes at a cost. I am on the road very early in the morning and don't come back until very late. Sometimes I go so far that I have to stay in a hotel overnight.

Sally: And it can be costly. He spends quite a bit of money while he's on the road. I keep track of his expenses, receipts, and mileage log. If the IRS ever audits us, we have the documentation for every dollar he spends.

Author: That's good. I see from your return that you receive a W-2 from your employer for the commission you make.

Sean: That's right. The more I'm on the road, the more money I make. Since our company doesn't reimburse my travel expenses, we deduct them from our taxes.

Author: I can see that. You deducted $47,000 as job-related expenses on your tax return.

Sally: Yes, I have all the documentation and receipts to prove that.

Author: That's great. In case if you ever get audited, you will have no problem.

Sally: What we really want, though, is to pay less in taxes. We paid nearly $16,000 in Alternate Minimum Tax last year, and I don't understand why. We don't mind paying our fair share in taxes, but why do we have to pay these additional taxes?

Author: I will explain that in a minute. Does your company offer 401(k) or any other retirement plans?

Sally: Yes, but we have been so busy that we never got a chance to complete the paperwork to enroll.

Author: Do they match your contributions?

Sally: Yes, they match 100 percent for up to 3 percent of our contributions.

Author: That 3 percent is like free money. Your contribution of 3 percent gets doubled overnight. Where else can you double your money in one day?

Sally: I know. I know. I'll make sure to complete the paperwork in a day or two and start contributing immediately.

Author: How much are you planning to contribute?

Sally: He is planning to contribute the full $18,000.

Author: That's great. It will also help you reduce your Alternate Minimum Tax slightly. But the major reason you are paying AMT is the job-related expenses you are deducting for Sean.

Sean: But those are legitimate expenses! If I don't spend that money, I don't make any money.

Author: I have absolutely no doubt about the legitimacy of those expenses, but the tax law works differently. You need to deduct those types of expenses as miscellaneous expenses on your Schedule A.

Sean: So what?

Author: Under the tax law, certain tax deductions can significantly reduce the regular tax. The AMT sets a limit on such deductions, and it confuses a lot of people. Deduction of your job-related expenses is not allowed under the AMT system. Basically, your taxes are calculated twice—once under the regular tax system and once under the AMT tax system.

If the calculations under the AMT system are higher than they are under the regular tax system, you need to pay the difference as AMT.

Sally: That's not fair. Is there something we can do about it?

Author: There is one way, but we need to involve Sean's employer.

Sean: What do they have to do with our AMT taxes?

Author: Instead of your deducting those expenses, why can't your employer reimburse you for them? They can reduce your commission to the extent of reimbursed expenses. That way, the employer is not spending any more money on you, but you get your W-2 with a smaller income.

Sean: How will that help us with our AMT taxes?

Author: Your W-2 income will be lower, because the reimbursement of your expenses will not be included in your W-2. Since you won't need to deduct job-related expenses on your tax return anymore, your AMT will either reduce or go away completely.

Sean: Really? Let me talk to my boss.

The next day, Sean's boss called me.

Boss: Sean told me about changing our accounting system. I didn't quite understand what he meant, but we can't change our accounting system.

I reviewed with him the conversation I'd had with Sean and Sally the previous day about how AMT works. I explained that the company did not have to change the complete accounting system.

Author: You simply have to create a reimbursement account for your employees and reduce the commission to that extent. The company will be paying the same amount to the employees, but instead of one check for a higher salary, you will be paying two checks. You'll have to pay one check for reimbursement of expenses and another for the reduced salary. That will make Sean's AMT go away.

Boss: Oh, now I understand the impact of job-related expenses on AMT. I'm also paying AMT but never quite understood it. If we change our accounting system for the reimbursement of job-related expenses, will my AMT also go away?

Author: Without looking at your tax situation, I can't say for sure, but if your job-related expenses are high, then your AMT could get reduced—if not completely eliminated.

Boss: That's great. Let me see what I can do.

A few days later, Sean and Sally came in to see me.

Sean: My employer agreed to reimburse my job-related expenses and reduce my commission by the same amount. Now we are ready for you to show us how it will reduce our taxes.

Author: I cannot change anything in your taxes for last year. It is too late for that, but I can show you what could happen next year, assuming your income and expenses remain the same.

I prepared another copy of the return, in which I took into account the effect of the new reimbursement plan and the reduced salary. I also took into account the $18,000 Sean would be contributing to their 401(k). At this point, I showed them the copy of the new projected tax return (figure 2-2).

Author: Look at line 45 of this new return for Alternate Minimum Tax. How much is it?

Sean: Zero. Does this mean no AMT?

Author: Yes, and now look at line 63 of your old return. What does it say?

Sally: $41,414

Author: That's your total federal tax liability for the previous year's return. Now look at the same line 63 in the new projected return. What does it say?

Sean: $20,638. Does that mean our taxes will go down from $41,414 to $20,638? That is a savings of more than $20,000! That will pay our 401(k) contributions. That means we'll be contributing $18,000 for our 401(k) and won't have to pay any new money out of pocket for it!

Author: That's correct. Instead of paying that amount to the IRS, you will be paying it to yourself for your retirement.

Sally: I can't believe that! On top of that, we will be getting free matching contributions from Sean's employer, so total savings will be many thousands more than $20,000.

Author: That's correct. Do you now believe in a second opinion when it comes to your taxes?

Sean: Are you kidding me? You have changed our lives.

Sally: I have a friend, Rhonda, whose husband, Ray, started a new business last year. They ended up paying a lot of money in taxes. Can I give your name to Rhonda?

Author: Sure. Our business depends on referrals. That's the way the business grew from one desk in the basement of my home to what it is today. I appreciate your referrals.

Sean: You deserve those referrals. We'll call our friends, Sam and Sonya, who referred us to you and thank them. I still can't believe the amount of money we will be saving year after year after year. Our taxes will be reduced by more than $20,000, and we will be investing $18,000 of that money in my retirement fund. In other words, I will be creating a free retirement for myself without coming up with any new money.

Sally: And the matching contribution from your employer will be the icing on the cake.

Author: Well, I wish you all the best. Continue working hard.

More and more people are getting into this Alternate Minimum Tax (AMT). In chapter 1, the IRS subjected Sam and Sonya to AMT because they were paying too much in state taxes. Sean and Sally, on the other hand, were subjected to AMT because they were deducting their legitimate job-related expenses. The following are some other factors that may affect the AMT system, depending on your situation:

1. Personal exemptions
2. Standard deductions
3. Medical deductions
4. Real-estate tax deductions
5. State-tax deductions
6. Depreciation deductions
7. State-tax refunds
8. Miscellaneous deductions on line 27 of Schedule A (Form 1040)
9. Investment interest expense deductions
10. Depletion deductions
11. Net operating loss deductions
12. Tax-exempt interest

13. Qualified small-business stocks
14. Exercise of incentive stock options
15. Gain or loss from disposition of property
16. Passive activities
17. Long-term contracts
18. Mining costs
19. Research and experimental costs
20. Intangible drilling costs

Bottom line: the AMT situation is very confusing. If you are subjected to AMT, you should seek help from a qualified professional who has experience in analyzing AMT calculations.

Harak Gala, CPA

Form 1040 — U.S. Individual Income Tax Return — 2015

Department of the Treasury — Internal Revenue Service (99)   OMB No. 1545-0074   IRS Use Only—Do not write or staple in this space.

For the year Jan. 1–Dec. 31, 2015, or other tax year beginning _____, 2015, ending _____, 20____   See separate instructions.

Your first name and initial: Sean   **Last name:** Taxpayer
Your social security number: 400-01-1003

If a joint return, spouse's first name and initial: Sally   **Last name:** Taxpayer
Spouse's social security number: 400-01-2003

Home address (number and street). If you have a P.O. box, see instructions. 456 Sales Street   **Apt. no.** ▲ Make sure the SSN(s) above and on line 6c are correct.

City, town or post office, state, and ZIP code. COLUMBIA MD 21045-

Presidential Election Campaign — Check here if you, or your spouse if filing jointly, want $3 to go to this fund. Checking a box below will not change your tax or refund. ☐ You ☐ Spouse

Foreign country name _____ Foreign province/state/county _____ Foreign postal code _____

Filing Status — Check only one box.
1. ☐ Single
2. ☒ Married filing jointly (even if only one had income)
3. ☐ Married filing separately. Enter spouse's SSN above and full name here ▶
4. ☐ Head of household (with qualifying person). (See instructions.) If the qualifying person is a child but not your dependent, enter this child's name here ▶
5. ☐ Qualifying widow(er) with dependent child

Exemptions
- 6a ☒ Yourself. If someone can claim you as a dependent, do not check box 6a
- 6b ☒ Spouse

Boxes checked on 6a and 6b: **2**

c Dependents:

(1) First name / Last name	(2) Dependent's social security number	(3) Dependent's relationship to you	(4) ✓ if child under age 17 qualifying for child tax credit
Lester Taxpayer	400-01-3003	SON	☒
Arthea Taxpayer	400-01-4003	DAUGHTER	☒

- No. of children on 6c who: lived with you: **2**
- did not live with you due to divorce or separation (see instructions): **0**
- Dependents on 6c not entered above: **0**

If more than four dependents, see instructions and check here ▶ ☐

d Total number of exemptions claimed .... Add numbers on lines above ▶ **4**

Income

Attach Form(s) W-2 here. Also attach Forms W-2G and 1099-R if tax was withheld.

If you did not get a W-2, see instructions.

7	Wages, salaries, tips, etc. Attach Form(s) W-2	226,000.
8a	Taxable interest. Attach Schedule B if required	1,250.
8b	Tax-exempt interest. Do not include on line 8a	
9a	Ordinary dividends. Attach Schedule B if required	5,000.
9b	Qualified dividends	1,000.
10	Taxable refunds, credits, or offsets of state and local income taxes	
11	Alimony received	
12	Business income or (loss). Attach Schedule C or C-EZ	
13	Capital gain or (loss). Attach Schedule D if required. If not required, check here ▶ ☒	19,000.
14	Other gains or (losses). Attach Form 4797	
15a	IRA distributions _____	b Taxable amount _____
16a	Pensions and annuities _____	b Taxable amount _____
17	Rental real estate, royalties, partnerships, S corporations, trusts, etc. Attach Schedule E	
18	Farm income or (loss). Attach Schedule F	
19	Unemployment compensation	
20a	Social security benefits _____	b Taxable amount _____
21	Other income. List type and amount	
22	Combine the amounts in the far right col. for lines 7 through 21. This is your **total income** ▶	251,250.

Adjusted Gross Income

23	Educator expenses	
24	Certain business expenses of reservists, performing artists, and fee-basis gov. officials. Attach Form 2106 or 2106-EZ	
25	Health savings account deduction. Attach Form 8889	
26	Moving expenses. Attach Form 3903	
27	Deductible part of self-employment tax. Attach Schedule SE	
28	Self-employed SEP, SIMPLE, and qualified plans	
29	Self-employed health insurance deduction	
30	Penalty on early withdrawal of savings	
31a	Alimony paid b Recipient's SSN ▶	
32	IRA deduction	
33	Student loan interest deduction	
34	Tuition and fees. Attach Form 8917	
35	Domestic production activities deduction. Attach Form 8903	
36	Add lines 23 through 35	
37	Subtract line 36 from line 22. This is your **adjusted gross income** ▶	251,250.

For Disclosure, Privacy Act, and Paperwork Reduction Act Notice, see separate instructions.   Form **1040** (2015)

BCA
Chapter 2-1 Page 1

Cut Your Tax In Half

Form 1040 (2015)   Sean & Sally Taxpayer   400-01-1003   Page **2**

Tax and Credits	38	Amount from line 37 (adjusted gross income)	38	251,250.
	39a	Check { ☐ You were born before Jan. 2, 1951, ☐ Blind. } Total boxes { ☐ Spouse was born before Jan. 2, 1951, ☐ Blind. } checked ▶ 39a		
Standard Deduction for—	b	If your spouse itemizes on a separate return or you were a dual-status alien, check here ▶ 39b ☐		
• People who check any box on line 39a or 39b or who can be claimed as a dependent, see instructions.	40	Itemized deductions (from Schedule A) or your standard deduction (see left margin)	40	87,750.
	41	Subtract line 40 from line 38	41	163,500.
	42	Exemptions. If line 38 is $154,950 or less, multiply $4,000 by the number on line 6d. Otherwise, see instructions	42	16,000.
	43	Taxable income. Subtract line 42 from line 41. If line 42 is more than line 41, enter -0-	43	147,500.
	44	Tax (see instructions). Check if any from: a ☐ Form(s) 8814 b ☐ Form 4972 c ☐	44	26,463.
• All others:	45	Alternative minimum tax (see instructions). Attach Form 6251	45	14,903.
Single or Married filing separately, $6,300	46	Excess advance premium tax credit repayment. Attach Form 8962	46	
	47	Add lines 44, 45, and 46 ▶	47	41,366.
Married filing jointly or Qualifying widow(er), $12,600	48	Foreign tax credit. Attach Form 1116 if required	48	
	49	Credit for child and dependent care expenses. Attach Form 2441	49	
	50	Education credits from Form 8863, line 19	50	
Head of household, $9,250	51	Retirement savings contributions credit. Attach Form 8880	51	
	52	Child tax credit. Attach Schedule 8812 if required	52	
	53	Residential energy credits. Attach Form 5695	53	
	54	Other credits from Form: a ☐ 3800 b ☐ 8801 c ☐	54	
	55	Add lines 48 through 54. These are your total credits	55	
	56	Subtract line 55 from line 47. If line 55 is more than line 47, enter -0- ▶	56	41,366.
Other Taxes	57	Self-employment tax. Attach Schedule SE	57	
	58	Unreported social security and Medicare tax from Form a ☐ 4137 b ☐ 8919	58	
	59	Additional tax on IRAs, other qualified retirement plans, etc. Attach Form 5329 if required	59	
	60a	Household employment taxes from Schedule H	60a	
	b	First-time homebuyer credit repayment. Attach Form 5405 if required	60b	
	61	Health care: individual responsibility (see instructions) Full-year coverage ☒	61	
	62	Taxes from: a ☐ Form 8959 b ☒ Form 8960 c ☐ instructions; enter code(s)	62	48.
	63	Add lines 56 through 62. This is your total tax ▶	63	41,414. Before
Payments	64	Federal income tax withheld from Forms W-2 and 1099	64	31,200.
If you have a qualifying child, attach Schedule EIC.	65	2015 estimated tax payments and amount applied from 2014 return	65	
	66a	Earned income credit (EIC)	66a	
	b	Nontaxable combat pay election	66b	
	67	Additional child tax credit. Attach Form 8812	67	
	68	American opportunity credit from Form 8863, line 8	68	
	69	Net premium tax credit. Attach Form 8962	69	
	70	Amount paid with request for extension to file	70	
	71	Excess social security and tier 1 RRTA tax withheld	71	
	72	Credit for federal tax on fuels. Attach Form 4136	72	
	73	Credits from Form: a ☐ 2439 b ☐ Reserved c ☐ 8885 d ☐	73	
	74	Add lines 64, 65, 66a, and 67 through 73. These are your total payments ▶	74	31,200.
Refund	75	If line 74 is more than line 63, subtract line 63 from line 74. This is the amount you overpaid	75	
	76a	Amount of line 75 you want refunded to you. If Form 8888 is attached, check here ▶ ☐	76a	
Direct deposit? See instructions.	b	Routing number		
	c	Type: ☐ Checking ☐ Savings		
	d	Account number		
	77	Amount of line 75 you want applied to your 2016 estimated tax ▶ 77		
Amount You Owe	78	Amount you owe. Subtract line 74 from line 63. For details on how to pay, see instructions ▶	78	10,349.
	79	Estimated tax penalty (see instructions)	79	135.
Third Party Designee	Do you want to allow another person to discuss this return with the IRS (see instructions)? ☒ Yes. Complete below. ☐ No			
	Designee's name ▶ Harak Gala CPA Phone no. ▶ 301-912-3450 Personal identification number (PIN) ▶ 52141			
Sign Here	Under penalties of perjury, I declare that I have examined this return and accompanying schedules and statements, and to the best of my knowledge and belief, they are true, correct, and complete. Declaration of preparer (other than taxpayer) is based on all information of which preparer has any knowledge.			
Joint return? See instructions. Keep a copy for your records.	Your signature Date Your occupation: Sales Daytime phone number			
	Spouse's signature. If a joint return, both must sign. Date Spouse's occupation: Homemaker If the IRS sent you an Identity Protection PIN, enter it here (see inst.)			
Paid Preparer Use Only	Print/Type preparer's name: Harak Gala CPA Preparer's signature: Harak Gala CPA Date: 10/23/2016 Check ☐ if self-employed PTIN: P01201430			
	Firm's name ▶ eTax Corporation Firm's EIN ▶ 52-1962613			
	Firm's address ▶ 727 Thornwood Dr ODENTON MD 21113 Phone no. 301-912-3450			

www.irs.gov/form1040   Form **1040** (2015)

Chapter 2-1 Page 2

Harak Gala, CPA

SCHEDULE A (Form 1040)
Department of the Treasury
Internal Revenue Service (99)

Itemized Deductions

▶ Information about Schedule A and its separate instructions is at www.irs.gov/schedulea.
▶ Attach to Form 1040.

OMB No. 1545-0074
2015
Attachment Sequence No. **07**

Name(s) shown on Form 1040: Sean & Sally Taxpayer
Your social security number: 400-01-1003

Section	Line	Description		Amount
Medical and Dental Expenses		Caution: Do not include expenses reimbursed or paid by others.		
	1	Medical and dental expenses (see instructions)	1	
	2	Enter amount from Form 1040, line 38	2	251,250.
	3	Multiply line 2 by 10% (.10). But if either you or your spouse was born before Jan. 2, 1951, multiply line 2 by 7.5% (.075) instead	3	25,125.
	4	Subtract line 3 from line 1. If line 3 is more than line 1, enter -0-	4	
Taxes You Paid	5	State and local (check only one box): a [X] Income taxes, or b [ ] General sales taxes	5	15,000.
	6	Real estate taxes (see instructions)	6	12,000.
	7	Personal property taxes	7	
	8	Other taxes. List type and amount ▶	8	
	9	Add lines 5 through 8	9	27,000.
Interest You Paid	10	Home mortgage interest and points reported to you on Form 1098	10	17,000.
Note: Your mortgage interest deduction may be limited (see instructions).	11	Home mortgage interest not reported to you on Form 1098. If paid to the person from whom you bought the home, see instructions and show that person's name, identifying no., and address ▶	11	
	12	Points not reported to you on Form 1098. See instructions for special rules	12	
	13	Mortgage insurance premiums (see instructions)	13	
	14	Investment interest. Attach Form 4952 if required. (See instructions.)	14	
	15	Add lines 10 through 14	15	17,000.
Gifts to Charity	16	Gifts by cash or check. If you made any gift of $250 or more, see instructions	16	1,200.
If you made a gift and got a benefit for it, see instructions.	17	Other than by cash or check. If any gift of $250 or more, see instructions. You must attach Form 8283 if over $500	17	500.
	18	Carryover from prior year	18	
	19	Add lines 16 through 18	19	1,700.
Casualty and Theft Losses	20	Casualty or theft loss(es). Attach Form 4684. (See instructions.)	20	
Job Expenses and Certain Miscellaneous Deductions	21	Unreimbursed employee expenses - job travel, union dues, job education, etc. Attach Form 2106 or 2106-EZ if required. (See instructions.) ▶	21	43,000.
	22	Tax preparation fees	22	395.
	23	Other expenses - investment, safe deposit box, etc. List type and amount ▶ Union Dues Investment Fees	23	3,680.
	24	Add lines 21 through 23	24	47,075.
	25	Enter amount from Form 1040, line 38	25	251,250.
	26	Multiply line 25 by 2% (.02)	26	5,025.
	27	Subtract line 26 from line 24. If line 26 is more than line 24, enter -0-	27	42,050.
Other Miscellaneous Deductions	28	Other - from list in the instr. List type and amount ▶	28	
Total Itemized Deductions	29	Is Form 1040, line 38, over $154,950? [X] No. Your deduction is not limited. Add the amounts in the far right column for lines 4 through 28. Also, enter this amount on Form 1040, line 40. [ ] Yes. Your deduction may be limited. See the Itemized Deductions Worksheet in the instructions to figure the amount to enter.	29	87,750.
	30	If you elect to itemize deductions even though they are less than your standard deduction, check here ▶ [ ]		

For Paperwork Reduction Act Notice, see Form 1040 instructions.
BCA

Schedule A (Form 1040) 2015

Chapter 2-1 Page 3

Cut Your Tax In Half

Form 1040 — U.S. Individual Income Tax Return — 2015

Taxpayer: Sean Taxpayer — SSN 400-02-1003
Spouse: Sally Taxpayer — SSN 400-01-2003
Address: 456 Sales Street, COLUMBIA MD 21045

Filing Status: 2 — Married filing jointly

Exemptions:
- 6a [X] Yourself
- 6b [X] Spouse
- Dependents:
  - Lester Taxpayer — 400-01-1003 — SON
  - Arthea Taxpayer — 400-01-4003 — DAUGHTER
- Total number of exemptions claimed: 4

Income:

Line	Description	Amount
7	Wages, salaries, tips, etc. Attach Form(s) W-2	161,000.
8a	Taxable interest. Attach Schedule B if required	1,250.
9a	Ordinary dividends. Attach Schedule B if required	5,000.
9b	Qualified dividends	1,000.
13	Capital gain or (loss). Attach Schedule D if required	19,000.
22	Combine the amounts in the far right column for lines 7 through 21. This is your **total income**	186,250.

Adjusted Gross Income:

Line	Description	Amount
36	Add lines 23 through 35	0.
37	Subtract line 36 from line 22. This is your **adjusted gross income**	186,250.

Form **1040** (2015)

Figure 2-2 Page 1

Figure 2-2 Page 2

Cut Your Tax In Half

SCHEDULE A (Form 1040)	Itemized Deductions	OMB No. 1545-0074 **2015**
Department of the Treasury Internal Revenue Service (99)	▶ Information about Schedule A and its separate instructions is at www.irs.gov/schedulea. ▶ Attach to Form 1040.	Attachment Sequence No. **07**
Name(s) shown on Form 1040 Sean & Sally Taxpayer		Your social security number 400-02-1083

Medical and Dental Expenses		Caution: Do not include expenses reimbursed or paid by others.			
	1	Medical and dental expenses (see instructions)	1		
	2	Enter amount from Form 1040, line 38	2	186,250.	
	3	Multiply line 2 by 10% (.10). But if either you or your spouse was born before Jan. 2, 1951, multiply line 2 by 7.5% (.075) instead	3	18,625.	
	4	Subtract line 3 from line 1. If line 3 is more than line 1, enter -0-			4
Taxes You Paid	5	State and local (check only one box): a [X] Income taxes, or b [ ] General sales taxes	5	15,000.	
	6	Real estate taxes (see instructions)	6	12,000.	
	7	Personal property taxes	7		
	8	Other taxes. List type and amount ▶	8		
	9	Add lines 5 through 8			9 27,000.
Interest You Paid	10	Home mortgage interest and points reported to you on Form 1098	10	17,000.	
Note: Your mortgage interest deduction may be limited (see instructions).	11	Home mortgage interest not reported to you on Form 1098. If paid to the person from whom you bought the home, see instructions and show that person's name, identifying no., and address ▶	11		
	12	Points not reported to you on Form 1098. See instructions for special rules.	12		
	13	Mortgage insurance premiums (see instructions)	13		
	14	Investment interest. Attach Form 4952 if required. (See instructions.)	14		
	15	Add lines 10 through 14			15 17,000.
Gifts to Charity	16	Gifts by cash or check. If you made any gift of $250 or more, see instructions.	16	1,200.	
If you made a gift and got a benefit for it, see instructions.	17	Other than by cash or check. If any gift of $250 or more, see instructions. You **must** attach Form 8283 if over $500	17	500.	
	18	Carryover from prior year	18		
	19	Add lines 16 through 18			19 1,700.
Casualty and Theft Losses	20	Casualty or theft loss(es). Attach Form 4684. (See instructions.)			20
Job Expenses and Certain Miscellaneous Deductions	21	Unreimbursed employee expenses - job travel, union dues, job education, etc. Attach Form 2106 or 2106-EZ if required. (See instructions.) ▶	21		
	22	Tax preparation fees	22	395.	
	23	Other expenses - investment, safe deposit box, etc. List type and amount ▶ Union Dues Investment Fees	23	3,680.	
	24	Add lines 21 through 23	24	4,075.	
	25	Enter amount from Form 1040, line 38	25	186,250.	
	26	Multiply line 25 by 2% (.02)	26	3,725.	
	27	Subtract line 26 from line 24. If line 26 is more than line 24, enter -0-			27 350.
Other Miscellaneous Deductions	28	Other - from list in the instructions. List type and amount ▶			28
Total Itemized Deductions	29	Is Form 1040, line 38, over $154,950? [X] **No.** Your deduction is not limited. Add the amounts in the far right column for lines 4 through 28. Also, enter this amount on Form 1040, line 40. [ ] **Yes.** Your deduction may be limited. See the Itemized Deductions Worksheet in the instructions to figure the amount to enter		▶	29 46,050.
	30	If you elect to itemize deductions even though they are less than your standard deduction, check here		▶ [ ]	

For Paperwork Reduction Act Notice, see Form 1040 instructions.   Schedule A (Form 1040) 2015

Figure 2-2 Page 3

Notes

Notes

CHAPTER 3

Business Entity

• • •

RAY WAS A MAINTENANCE WORKER. His wife, Rhonda, was attending community college. They had two children, ages six and eight years old. Ray was earning $40,000 a year and struggling to maintain his household on that salary. He'd tried to get another job with a higher salary, but it was difficult to get more money in his field. After talking to his wife, he decided to start his own business. They had heard from friends that it would be better to start the business as an LLC, to limit their personal liabilities.

As their friends suggested, Ray and Rhonda used the Internet to form the company. It was an easy and cheap process. They found a website that could form an LLC for them and submitted the required information online. The site formed a single-member LLC quickly, and Ray and Rhonda couldn't have been more excited. After all, Ray had good experience in his field, and he knew many people who could help him get more work.

During the company's first year of operation, Ray made a profit of $86,000 after deducting all his business expenses. He and Rhonda were happy with the results. At the end of the year, they submitted their information to their tax preparer. In the past, they had always received a sizable refund. They were getting child tax credit for their two young children and also getting college credit for Rhonda. Since Rhonda was going to college two days each week, they had to pay a day-care provider for the children's care. This gave them a dependent-care credit on their taxes as well. This year they were hoping all these credits would offset the additional taxes due on their higher income.

They submitted all the details of their income and expenses to the tax preparer, and a week later, they went to pick up their completed return. When they looked at the return, they couldn't believe it—they owed $11,690 in federal taxes. They thought something was wrong with their tax return (shown in figure 3-1).

Rhonda: What about the credit for the day-care expenses?

Tax Preparer: Look at line 49 of your 1040. There's a credit of $1,200 for the day-care expenses.

Rhonda: What about my college credit?

Tax Preparer: Look at lines 50 and 68. You get a total of $2,500 in education credits.

Ray: What about the tax credit for our children? Don't we get a lot of money for our children?

Tax Preparer: Yes, you do. Look at line 52. There is a child tax credit for $2,000. In all, you get total credits of $5,700. Your federal income tax on line 47 is $5,194.

Ray: So our credit amount is larger than our income tax. Shouldn't we get a refund then?

Tax Preparer: Yes, your credit amount is larger than the federal income tax, and you could get a refund if there was no self-employment tax due. Look at line 57 of your tax return. The self-employment tax is $12,151. Your total tax bill is $11,855. So if there was no self-employment tax, you would get a small refund. But as per the law, you have to pay self-employment tax.

Ray and Rhonda: We do not have that kind of money. We can pay half the amount, but we do not have the money for the other half. What can we do?

Tax Preparer: I can make a request for a payment plan. You can pay half now, and the rest can be paid in monthly installments. The IRS will charge you $120 for setting up the payment plan and also some interest on the balance.

Ray: Geez. We have no choice but to arrange a payment plan.

All the excitement of starting the new business disappeared, but going back to that $40,000 job was not an option. They had confidence in their tax preparer. After all, he had explained to them line by line why they owed money. Seeing this wasn't going to change the tax laws. They assumed that when you make more money, you have to pay more taxes. (If that were true, some big companies would not be paying zero taxes in spite of making huge profits). At that point, Ray and Rhonda were referred to us for a second opinion. Reluctantly, they agreed to see me.

I looked at their return. It was 100 percent accurate.

Author: Your tax preparer has done a good job in preparing your tax return.

Ray: He has been doing our taxes ever since I started working. He has never been wrong even once. I know nothing can be changed, and I am sorry to waste your time.

Author: Wait a minute. I am not done. Can I ask you a few questions?

Rhonda: Go on.

Author: Why did you form an LLC?

Ray: Isn't that the best option? We wanted to limit our liability. It was so easy to go on the Internet and form the LLC. It didn't even cost much.

Author: LLC is definitely a good option in certain circumstances. It may or may not be the best option in other situations. It all depends on your goals, circumstances, and requirements.

Ray: Right now, the only thing we are worried about is taxes.

Author: Before you start any business, you need to do some initial planning and may need some help from a professional. Did the people who helped you form the business help you in determining your priorities?

Ray: We did it online. We told them what we wanted. There was no counseling from anybody.

Author: Did you consider forming an S corporation instead of an LLC?

Ray: Does it provide liability protection?

Author: Yes, it does provide liability protection, if you do everything properly. S corporation formation has its limitations and is not ideal in all situations, but in your circumstances, it could reduce your tax burden.

Ray: Really? How?

Author: If you were to do the same kind of work for somebody else, how much could you expect as salary?

Ray: Maximum $40,000.

Author: Suppose we convert your business to an S corporation, and you take a salary of $43,000 from your company. Would that salary be considered reasonable, based on the market rates?

Ray: It would be more than reasonable.

Author: So let's look at your tax return again. After all the expenses, your profit was $86,000. You did not pay any regular income tax, because you had many tax credits to offset your regular income tax. But you ended up paying $12,151 in self-employment tax. Is that correct?

Rhonda: Yes. If self-employment tax were not there, we would have received a small refund.

Author: Suppose you form an S corporation and Ray pays himself a salary of $43,000. The self-employment tax will be reduced by half. It would be $6,579. You could withdraw the rest of the profit without paying any self-employment tax. Your income would not get reduced, but your taxes would be reduced by nearly 50 percent.

Rhonda: That means if we had formed an S corporation instead of an LLC, we would not need any payment plan and would be debt-free from the IRS. We should have consulted you before we started our business.

Author: It is not too late. But before we do that, let's discuss other characteristics of an S corporation. After that if you decide to change your company to be taxed as an S corporation, we can do that.

I discussed with them the advantages and limitations of different business entities, including those of S corporations. I also explained to them the requirements from the IRS for filing business tax returns. After listening to their options, they decided to change their tax status to an S corporation to reduce their self-employment tax in half. After all, starting the business was not a bad idea.

Ray: We also know that you are doing financial planning. Unfortunately, we don't have much savings right now.

Author: Don't worry. The way you doubled your income gives me a lot of confidence in your abilities. After Rhonda finishes her schooling, she will also start working. You will make a lot of money. Soon, you will need help with college planning for your children. As your business grows, we will have to incorporate retirement planning as a part of the tax-planning process. We will work together on all these issues. Tax planning is not a one-time process. It is an ongoing process. As you start making more money, there are more tax planning and financial planning opportunities available to you.

Rhonda: I am so relieved. Can I ask you one more question?
Author: Sure.
Rhonda: My parents are retired. They are not making much but still pay a lot of taxes. Can you see them?
Author: Sure. They will need to bring their latest financial statements and their tax returns for the previous two years.
Rhonda: Thank you for everything.

NOTE: No single type of entity is ideal in all situations. Every type has some advantages and some disadvantages. There may be certain legal considerations that may outweigh tax consideration. Also, in certain situations, another entity type may have better tax advantages. It is a good idea to take advice from both a tax and legal professional before you start a new business.

Cut Your Tax In Half

Form 1040 U.S. Individual Income Tax Return 2015

Name: Ray Taxpayer
Spouse: Rhonda Taxpayer
SSN: 400-01-1004
Spouse SSN: 400-01-2004
Address: 123 Construction Street
City: COLUMBIA MD 21045-

Filing Status: 2 — Married filing jointly

Exemptions:
- 6a [X] Yourself
- 6b [X] Spouse
- Dependents:
  - Robin Taxpayer, 400-01-3003, DAUGHTER
  - Rik Taxpayer, 400-01-4003, SON
- Total number of exemptions claimed: 4

Income

Line	Description	Amount
12	Business income or (loss). Attach Schedule C or C-EZ	86,000.
22	Total income	86,000.

Adjusted Gross Income

Line	Description	Amount
27	Deductible part of self-employment tax. Attach Schedule SE	6,076.
36	Add lines 23 through 35	6,076.
37	Subtract line 36 from line 22. This is your **adjusted gross income**	79,924.

Form **1040** (2015)

Figure 3-1 Page 1

Harak Gala, CPA

Form 1040 (2015)   Ray & Rhonda Taxpayer   400-01-1004   Page **2**

Tax and Credits	38 Amount from line 37 (adjusted gross income)	38	79,924.
	39a Check: You were born before Jan. 2, 1951, [ ] Blind. Total boxes Spouse was born before Jan. 2, 1951, [ ] Blind. checked ▶ 39a [ ]		
Standard Deduction for—	b If your spouse itemizes on a separate return or you were a dual-status alien, check here ▶ 39b [ ]		
• People who check any box on line 39a or 39b or who can be claimed as a dependent, see instructions.	40 **Itemized deductions** (from Schedule A) or your **standard deduction** (see left margin)	40	23,150.
	41 Subtract line 40 from line 38	41	56,774.
	42 Exemptions. If line 38 is $154,950 or less, multiply $4,000 by the number on line 6d. Otherwise, see instructions	42	16,000.
	43 **Taxable income.** Subtract line 42 from line 41. If line 42 is more than line 41, enter -0-	43	40,774.
	44 Tax (see instructions). Check if any from: a [ ] Form(s) 8814 b [ ] Form 4972 c [ ]	44	5,194.
• All others Single or Married filing separately, $6,300	45 Alternative minimum tax (see instructions). Attach Form 6251	45	
	46 Excess advance premium tax credit repayment. Attach Form 8962	46	
	47 Add lines 44, 45, and 46 ▶	47	5,194.
Married filing jointly or Qualifying widow(er), $12,600	48 Foreign tax credit. Attach Form 1116 if required	48	
	49 Credit for child and dependent care expenses. Attach Form 2441	49	1,200.
	50 Education credits from Form 8863, line 19	50	1,500.
Head of household, $9,250	51 Retirement savings contributions credit. Attach Form 8880	51	
	52 Child tax credit. Attach Schedule 8812, if required	52	2,000.
	53 Residential energy credits. Attach Form 5695	53	
	54 Other credits from Form: a [ ] 3800 b [ ] 8801 c [ ]	54	
	55 Add lines 48 through 54. These are your **total credits**	55	4,700.
	56 Subtract line 55 from line 47. If line 55 is more than line 47, enter -0- ▶	56	494.
Other Taxes	57 Self-employment tax. Attach Schedule SE	57	12,151. Before
	58 Unreported social security and Medicare tax from Form a [ ] 4137 b [ ] 8919	58	
	59 Additional tax on IRAs, other qualified retirement plans, etc. Attach Form 5329 if required	59	
	60a Household employment taxes from Schedule H	60a	
	b First-time homebuyer credit repayment. Attach Form 5405 if required	60b	
	61 Health care: individual responsibility (see instructions) Full-year coverage [ ]	61	
	62 Taxes from: a [ ] Form 8959 b [ ] Form 8960 c [ ] instructions; enter code(s)	62	
	63 Add lines 56 through 62. This is your **total tax** ▶	63	12,645.
Payments	64 Federal income tax withheld from Forms W-2 and 1099	64	
If you have a qualifying child, attach Schedule EIC.	65 2015 estimated tax payments and amount applied from 2014 return	65	
	66a Earned income credit (EIC)	66a	
	b Nontaxable combat pay election 66b		
	67 Additional child tax credit. Attach Form 8812	67	
	68 American opportunity credit from Form 8863, line 8	68	1,000.
	69 Net premium tax credit. Attach Form 8962	69	
	70 Amount paid with request for extension to file	70	
	71 Excess social security and tier 1 RRTA tax withheld	71	
	72 Credit for federal tax on fuels. Attach Form 4136	72	
	73 Credits from Form: a [ ] 2439 b [ ] Reserved c [ ] 8885 d [ ]	73	
	74 Add lines 64, 65, 66a, and 67 through 73. These are your **total payments** ▶	74	1,000.
Refund	75 If line 74 is more than line 63, subtract line 63 from line 74. This is the amount you **overpaid**	75	
	76a Amount of line 75 you want **refunded to you.** If Form 8888 is attached, check here ▶ [ ]	76a	
Direct deposit? See instructions.	b Routing number c Type: [ ] Checking [ ] Savings		
	d Account number		
	77 Amount of line 75 you want applied to your 2016 **estimated tax** ▶ 77		
Amount You Owe	78 **Amount you owe.** Subtract line 74 from line 63. For details on how to pay, see instructions ▶	78	11,645.
	79 Estimated tax penalty (see instructions) 79	210.	
Third Party Designee	Do you want to allow another person to discuss this return with the IRS (see instructions)? [X] **Yes.** Complete below. [ ] No Designee's name ▶ Harak Gala CPA Phone no. ▶ 301-912-3450 Personal identification number (PIN) ▶ 62341		
Sign Here	Under penalties of perjury, I declare that I have examined this return and accompanying schedules and statements, and to the best of my knowledge and belief, they are true, correct, and complete. Declaration of preparer (other than taxpayer) is based on all information of which preparer has any knowledge.		
Joint return? See instructions. Keep a copy for your records.	Your signature Date Your occupation Construction Manager Daytime phone number		
	Spouse's signature. If a joint return, **both** must sign. Date Spouse's occupation Student If the IRS sent you an Identity Protection PIN, enter it here		
Paid Preparer Use Only	Print/Type preparer's name Harak Gala CPA Preparer's signature Harak Gala CPA Date 10/23/2016 Check [ ] if self-employed PTIN P01201436		
	Firm's name ▶ eTax Corporation Firm's EIN ▶ 52-1963619		
	Firm's address ▶ 727 Thornwood Dr ODENTON MD 21113 Phone no. 301-912-3450		

www.irs.gov/form1040   BCA   Form **1040** (2015)

Figure 3-1 Page 2

Notes

Notes

CHAPTER 4

Change of Profession

● ● ●

MARK AND MARY WERE FRUSTRATED with their taxes. In 2006 and 2007, they purchased two rental properties at substantially high prices. In 2008–2009, the prices of those properties went down considerably. The new market value was a lot less than the mortgage balance. The rental income was not enough to cover their mortgage payments, but they had no choice but to continue. Selling was not an option. To add insult to injury, they were not able to deduct the rental losses from their taxes.

Mark was earning $140,000 working as a construction manager. In the past, Mary had had a real-estate business and used to make good money. But after the economic downturn of 2008, she was not able to do much business. She did get contracts on a few houses, but the buyer's loans did not go through. She had no choice but to quit as a real-estate agent. One of her friends gave her the idea of starting a multilevel marketing business. She was working very hard but was not able to make much money. All the money she was making in her business was being used in maintaining the two rental properties. She had to pay taxes on whatever little money she was making in her business, and they were not able to deduct any losses from their rental properties.

At this point, Mark and Mary were referred to our company by an existing client. As usual, any new prospects we see for the first time are asked to bring their tax returns for the previous two years, along with their latest financial statements. Before I looked at their tax return, I inquired about their background.

Mark: We are generating a huge loss from our rental properties, but our tax preparer is telling us we cannot deduct the losses on our tax return.

Author: Did you discuss this with your tax preparer?

Mark: You bet we did. She told us we are making too much money. By law, the rental real-estate activity generally is considered passive activity. If our adjusted gross income is more than $150,000, then we cannot deduct passive-activity losses.

Author: She is absolutely right.

Mark: That means we cannot do anything but keep on paying these taxes. I make only $140,000, and I work very hard for it. Mary hardly makes anything. In today's economy, that is not much money. We barely get by on the money we earn. We pay taxes on the money we earn but can't deduct our losses, even though part of the money we earn is used for those losses. That's not fair.

Author: Can I look at your tax return?

Mary: Absolutely. Here's a copy of our tax return (shown in figure 4-1).

Author: Mary, I see here that you are self-employed.

Mary: I am a multilevel marketer and do door-to-door sales. I don't like it. In the past I was a real-estate agent, but it was tough to stay in the business during the economic downturn of 2008 and 2009. I loved being a real-estate agent, and I was doing very well before 2008. After 2008 the buyers were simply not qualifying for the loans. After doing all the work and getting buyers to sign the contract, it was so frustrating to see buyers unable to get the loans. It became too hard to meet the expenses of the real-estate office.

Author: How is the real-estate market now?

Mary: Not too bad, and it seems to be improving.

Author: Would you like to go back to that business again?

Mary: I would love it, but getting back into it is not that easy. Going through the licensing and establishing the real-estate office again is an involved process.

Author: Hmmm. Let's take a look at your tax return. Assume you were a real-estate agent instead of a multilevel marketer last year. Let us further assume that you made the same amount of money in the real-estate business instead of the multilevel marketing business.

Mary: What difference does it make? It will be the same amount of income, whether I am in the real-estate business or the multilevel marketing business.

Author: As long as you spend a majority of your working hours performing qualified real-estate activities and those hours add up to at least 750 during the year, you are considered a real-estate professional per the guidelines from the IRS.

Mary: But I still don't understand. What difference does it make?

Author: If you are a real-estate professional, you can deduct rental losses of up to $25,000. Real-estate professionals are allowed to deduct rental losses irrespective of their income. Let me quickly run some numbers. That may allow you to deduct your real-estate losses, and your tax liability would change from $24,589 to $12,886.

The copy of the tax return is shown in figure 4-2.

Mark: What? Let's redo our last year's tax return!

Author: Unfortunately, we cannot change last year's tax return. Mary was not a real-estate professional last year.

To be a real-estate professional, an individual must spend the majority of his or her time in real property businesses:

1. Development or redevelopment
2. Construction or reconstruction
3. Acquisition or conversion
4. Rental
5. Management or operation
6. Leasing

The taxpayer must meet each of the following time requirements:

1. More than 50 percent of his or her time is spent working in real property businesses, and
2. More than 750 hours of service during the year.

One spouse alone must meet both obligations. In addition, services performed as an employee do not count unless the employee is at least a 5 percent owner.

Finally, before rental losses are deductible without being limited by the passive-losses rules, the taxpayer must materially participate in each rental.

Mary: I can do that! Satisfying those conditions is a not a problem. I will start working on my real-estate license tomorrow.

Mark: That means we won't owe any taxes next year. Am I right?

Author: It looks like Mary loves the real-estate business. She might make a lot more money than what she is making now. If that happens, your taxes could increase.

Mark: We don't mind paying more taxes if we make more money. We just don't like paying taxes when we lose money.

Mary: And as we make more money, you will help us in implementing more tax-savings strategies, won't you?

Author: Sure. It is your right to use legal tax-savings strategies.

Mark: We aren't going anywhere else. You will be the first to know as we start making more money!

Mark and Mary had problems because they lost money in real-estate activities.

Now, take the example of John and Jenny. They rented out their old house for many years, and it was fully depreciated. They had purchased it at a very low price, and over time and with market increases, they'd seen a substantial gain in the value of that property. But the old house was taking up a significant amount of their time. They wanted to sell and were afraid of paying capital-gain taxes and depreciation-recapture taxes. They preferred the idea of owning a newer, low-maintenance property but were avoiding making any actual changes because of taxes.

A simple solution for them would be to use the law of *1031* exchange. They could sell the old house and use that money to buy another house of equal or greater value using *1031* regulations. If done properly, all their federal and state capital-gain tax, including depreciation recapture, could be deferred until they sold this second house. If they never sold this second house and instead passed it on to their kids, the kids would get a step-up in basis on this house. The children could then sell this house immediately after the death of their second parent and would not pay any taxes. With proper planning, a taxpayer can do multiple *1031* exchanges during his or her lifetime and never pay capital-gain taxes. If he or she needs money while alive, he or she can borrow against the property but not sell the last house during his or her lifetime. This is an excellent way of converting taxable capital gain from an investment into a tax-free investment with no federal or state income-tax liabilities.

Harak Gala, CPA

Form 1040 — U.S. Individual Income Tax Return — **2015**

OMB No. 1545-0074

For the year Jan. 1-Dec. 31, 2015, or other tax year beginning _____, 2015, ending _____, 20 ____

Your first name and initial: **Mark** Last name: **Taxpayer**
Your social security number: **400-01-1005**

If a joint return, spouse's first name and initial: **Mary** Last name: **Taxpayer**
Spouse's social security number: **400-01-2005**

Home address (number and street): **123 Main Street**

City, town or post office, state, and ZIP code: **COLUMBIA MD 21045**

Filing Status
2. [X] Married filing jointly (even if only one had income)

Exemptions
- 6a [X] Yourself
- 6b [X] Spouse
- Boxes checked on 6a and 6b: **2**
- Total number of exemptions claimed: **2**

Income

7	Wages, salaries, tips, etc. Attach Form(s) W-2	140,000.
8a	Taxable interest. Attach Schedule B if required	500.
8b	Tax-exempt interest	
9a	Ordinary dividends. Attach Schedule B if required	950.
9b	Qualified dividends	100.
12	Business income or (loss). Attach Schedule C or C-EZ	12,900.
13	Capital gain or (loss). Attach Schedule D [X]	2,700.
22	**Total income**	157,050.

Adjusted Gross Income

Line	Description	Amount
27	Deductible part of self-employment tax. Attach Schedule SE	911.
36	Add lines 23 through 35	911.
37	Subtract line 36 from line 22. This is your **adjusted gross income**	156,139.

Figure 4-1 Page 1

Form **1040** (2015)

Cut Your Tax In Half

Form 1040 (2015)	Mark & Mary Taxpayer		400-01-1005		Page **2**
Tax and Credits	38 Amount from line 37 (adjusted gross income)			38	156,139.
	39a Check ☐ You were born before Jan. 2, 1951, ☐ Blind. ☐ Spouse was born before Jan. 2, 1951, ☐ Blind. } Total boxes checked ▶ 39a ☐				
Standard Deduction for—	b If your spouse itemizes on a separate return or you were a dual-status alien, check here ▶ 39b ☐				
• People who check any box on line 39a or 39b or who can be claimed as a dependent, see instructions.	40 Itemized deductions (from Schedule A) or your standard deduction (see left margin)			40	22,300.
	41 Subtract line 40 from line 38			41	133,839.
	42 Exemptions. If line 38 is $154,950 or less, multiply $4,000 by the number on line 6d. Otherwise, see instructions			42	8,000.
	43 Taxable income. Subtract line 42 from line 41. If line 42 is more than line 41, enter -0-			43	125,839.
• All others: Single or Married filing separately, $6,300	44 Tax (see instructions). Check if any from: a ☐ Form(s) 8814 b ☐ Form 4972 c ☐			44	22,767.
	45 Alternative minimum tax (see instructions). Attach Form 6251			45	
Married filing jointly or Qualifying widow(er), $12,600	46 Excess advance premium tax credit repayment. Attach Form 8962			46	
	47 Add lines 44, 45, and 46			▶ 47	22,767.
	48 Foreign tax credit. Attach Form 1116 if required	48			
Head of household, $9,250	49 Credit for child and dependent care expenses. Attach Form 2441	49			
	50 Education credits from Form 8863, line 19	50			
	51 Retirement savings contributions credit. Attach Form 8880	51			
	52 Child tax credit. Attach Schedule 8812, if required	52			
	53 Residential energy credits. Attach Form 5695	53			
	54 Other credits from Form: a ☐ 3800 b ☐ 8801 c ☐	54			
	55 Add lines 48 through 54. These are your total credits			55	
	56 Subtract line 55 from line 47. If line 55 is more than line 47, enter -0-			▶ 56	22,767.
Other Taxes	57 Self-employment tax. Attach Schedule SE			57	1,822.
	58 Unreported social security and Medicare tax from Form a ☐ 4137 b ☐ 8919			58	
	59 Additional tax on IRAs, other qualified retirement plans, etc. Attach Form 5329 if required			59	
	60a Household employment taxes from Schedule H			60a	
	b First-time homebuyer credit repayment. Attach Form 5405 if required			60b	
	61 Health care: individual responsibility (see instructions) Full-year coverage ☒			61	
	62 Taxes from: a ☐ Form 8959 b ☐ Form 8960 c ☐ instructions; enter code(s)			62	
	63 Add lines 56 through 62. This is your total tax			▶ 63	24,589. Before
Payments	64 Federal income tax withheld from Forms W-2 and 1099	64	18,000.		
If you have a qualifying child, attach Schedule EIC.	65 2015 estimated tax payments and amount applied from 2014 return	65			
	66a Earned income credit (EIC)	66a			
	b Nontaxable combat pay election 66b				
	67 Additional child tax credit. Attach Form 8812	67			
	68 American opportunity credit from Form 8863, line 8	68			
	69 Net premium tax credit. Attach Form 8962	69			
	70 Amount paid with request for extension to file	70			
	71 Excess social security and tier 1 RRTA tax withheld	71			
	72 Credit for federal tax on fuels. Attach Form 4136	72			
	73 Credits from Form: a ☐ 2439 b ☐ Reserved c ☐ 8885 d ☐	73			
	74 Add lines 64, 65, 66a, and 67 through 73. These are your total payments			▶ 74	18,000.
Refund	75 If line 74 is more than line 63, subtract line 63 from line 74. This is the amount you overpaid			75	
	76a Amount of line 75 you want refunded to you. If Form 8888 is attached, check here ▶ ☐			76a	
Direct deposit? See instructions.	▶ b Routing number ▶ c Type: ☐ Checking ☐ Savings				
	▶ d Account number				
	77 Amount of line 75 you want applied to your 2016 estimated tax ▶	77			
Amount You Owe	78 Amount you owe. Subtract line 74 from line 63. For details on how to pay, see instructions			▶ 78	6,672.
	79 Estimated tax penalty (see instructions)	79	83.		
Third Party Designee	Do you want to allow another person to discuss this return with the IRS (see instructions)? ☒ **Yes.** Complete below. ☐ No				
	Designee's name ▶ Hayak Gala CPA Phone no. ▶ 301-912-3456 Personal identification number (PIN) ▶ 32341				
Sign Here Joint return? See instructions. Keep a copy for your records.	Your signature Date Your occupation Construction Manager Daytime phone number				
	Spouse's signature. If a joint return, both must sign. Date Spouse's occupation Self Employed				
Paid Preparer Use Only	Print/Type preparer's name Hayak Gala CPA Preparer's signature Hayak Gala CPA Date 10/23/2016 Check ☐ if self-employed PTIN P01201436				
	Firm's name ▶ eTax Corporation Firm's EIN ▶ 52-1942629				
	Firm's address ▶ 727 Thornwood Dr ODENTON MD 21113 Phone no. 301-912-3456				
www.irs.gov/form1040 BCA					Form **1040** (2015)

Figure 4-1 Page 2

Harak Gala, CPA

SCHEDULE E (Form 1040) Department of the Treasury Internal Revenue Service	Supplemental Income and Loss (From rental real estate, royalties, partnerships, S corporations, estates, trusts, REMICs, etc.) ▶ Attach to Form 1040, 1040NR, or Form 1041. ▶ Information about Schedule E and its separate instructions is at www.irs.gov/schedulee.	OMB No. 1545-0074 **2015** Attachment Sequence No. **13**

Name(s) shown on return: **Mark & Mary Taxpayer**
Your social security no.: **400-01-1005**

Part I — Income or Loss From Rental Real Estate and Royalties
Note: If you are in the business of renting personal property, use Schedule C or C-EZ (see instructions). If you are an individual, report farm rental income or loss from **Form 4835** on page 2, line 40.

A Did you make any payments in 2015 that would require you to file Form(s) 1099? (see instructions) — Yes [X] No
B If "Yes," did you or will you file all required Forms 1099? — Yes [ ] No [ ]

1a Physical address of each property (street, city, state, Zip code)
A 123 Rental Way
B 456 Rental Street
C

1b Type of Property (from list below)	2 For each rental real estate property listed above, report the number of fair rental and personal use days. Check the QJV box only if you meet the requirements to file as a qualified joint venture. See instructions.		Fair Rental Days	Personal Use Days	QJV
A 2		A	365		[ ]
B 2		B	365		[ ]
C		C			[ ]

Type of Property:
1 Single Family Residence   3 Vacation/Short-Term Rental   5 Land   7 Self-Rental
2 Multi-Family Residence   4 Commercial   6 Royalties   8 Other (describe)

Income:	Properties:		A	B	C
3 Rents received		3	15,000.	18,000.	
4 Royalties received		4			
Expenses:					
5 Advertising		5			
6 Auto and travel (see instructions)		6	140.	280.	
7 Cleaning and maintenance		7	500.	750.	
8 Commissions		8			
9 Insurance		9	780.	840.	
10 Legal and other professional fees		10			
11 Management fees		11			
12 Mortgage interest paid to banks, etc. (see instructions)		12	15,500.	18,000.	
13 Other interest		13			
14 Repairs		14	2,980.	3,750.	
15 Supplies		15			
16 Taxes		16	4,000.	5,000.	
17 Utilities		17			
18 Depreciation expense or depletion		18	13,457.	13,817.	
19 Other (list) ▶		19			
20 Total expenses. Add lines 5 through 19		20	37,357.	42,437.	
21 Subtract line 20 from line 3 (rents) and/or 4 (royalties). If result is a (loss), see instructions to find out if you must file **Form 6198**		21	(22,357.)	(24,437.)	
22 Deductible rental real estate loss after limitation, if any, on **Form 8582** (see instructions)		22	( )	( )	( )
23a Total of all amounts reported on line 3 for all rental properties		23a	33,000.		
b Total of all amounts reported on line 4 for all royalty properties		23b			
c Total of all amounts reported on line 12 for all properties		23c	33,500.		
d Total of all amounts reported on line 18 for all properties		23d	27,274.		
e Total of all amounts reported on line 20 for all properties		23e	79,794.		
24 **Income.** Add positive amounts shown on line 21. **Do not** include any losses				24	
25 **Losses.** Add royalty losses from line 21 and rental real estate losses from line 22. Enter total losses here				25 (	)
26 **Total rental real estate and royalty income or (loss).** Combine lines 24 and 25. Enter the result here. If Parts II, III, IV, and line 40 on page 2 do not apply to you, also enter this amount on Form 1040, line 17, or Form 1040NR, line 18. Otherwise, include this amount in the total on line 41 on page 2				26	0

For Paperwork Reduction Act Notice, see the separate instructions.   Schedule E (Form 1040) 2015

BCA

Figure 4-1 Page 3

Cut Your Tax In Half

Form **1040**	Department of the Treasury — Internal Revenue Service (99) U.S. Individual Income Tax Return	**2015**	OMB No. 1545-0074	IRS Use Only—Do not write or staple in this space.

For the year Jan. 1–Dec. 31, 2015, or other tax year beginning _____, 2015, ending _____, 20___ See separate instructions.

Your first name and initial	Last name	Your social security number
Mark Taxpayer		400-02-1005
If a joint return, spouse's first name and initial	Last name	Spouse's social security number
Mary Taxpayer		400-01-2005

Home address (number and street). If you have a P.O. box, see instructions. Apt. no.
123 Main Street

▲ Make sure the SSN(s) above and on line 6c are correct.

City, town or post office, state, and ZIP code. If you have a foreign address, also complete spaces below (see instructions).
COLUMBIA MD 21045-

Presidential Election Campaign
Check here if you, or your spouse if filing jointly, want $3 to go to this fund. Checking a box below will not change your tax or refund. ☐ You ☐ Spouse

Foreign country name _____ Foreign province/state/county _____ Foreign postal code _____

Filing Status
Check only one box.
1. ☐ Single
2. ☒ Married filing jointly (even if only one had income)
3. ☐ Married filing separately. Enter spouse's SSN above and full name here. ▶
4. ☐ Head of household (with qualifying person). (See instructions.) If the qualifying person is a child but not your dependent, enter this child's name here. ▶
5. ☐ Qualifying widow(er) with dependent child

Exemptions
- 6a ☒ Yourself. If someone can claim you as a dependent, **do not** check box 6a ..... } Boxes checked on 6a and 6b **2**
- b ☒ Spouse .....
- c Dependents:
  - (1) First name Last name
  - (2) Dependent's social security number
  - (3) Dependent's relationship to you
  - (4) ☐ if child under age 17 qualifying for child tax credit (see instructions)

If more than four dependents, see instructions and check here ▶ ☐

- No. of children on 6c who:
  - lived with you **0**
  - did not live with you due to divorce or separation (see instructions) **0**
- Dependents on 6c not entered above **0**
- Add numbers on lines above ▶ **2**

d Total number of exemptions claimed

Income
Attach Form(s) W-2 here. Also attach Forms W-2G and 1099-R if tax was withheld.

If you did not get a W-2, see instructions.

7	Wages, salaries, tips, etc. Attach Form(s) W-2	7	140,000.
8a	Taxable interest. Attach Schedule B if required	8a	500.
b	Tax-exempt interest. **Do not** include on line 8a	8b	
9a	Ordinary dividends. Attach Schedule B if required	9a	950.
b	Qualified dividends	9b	100.
10	Taxable refunds, credits, or offsets of state and local income taxes	10	
11	Alimony received	11	
12	Business income or (loss). Attach Schedule C or C-EZ	12	12,900.
13	Capital gain or (loss). Attach Schedule D if required. If not required, check here ▶ ☒	13	2,700.
14	Other gains or (losses). Attach Form 4797	14	
15a	IRA distributions	15a	b Taxable amount	15b	
16a	Pensions and annuities	16a	b Taxable amount	16b	
17	Rental real estate, royalties, partnerships, S corporations, trusts, etc. Attach Schedule E	17	(40,794.)
18	Farm income or (loss). Attach Schedule F	18	
19	Unemployment compensation	19	
20a	Social security benefits	20a	b Taxable amount	20b	
21	Other income. List type and amount	21	
22	Combine the amounts in the far right column for lines 7 through 21. This is your **total income** ▶	22	116,256.

Adjusted Gross Income

23	Educator expenses	23	
24	Certain business expenses of reservists, performing artists, and fee-basis gov. officials. Attach Form 2106 or 2106-EZ	24	
25	Health savings account deduction. Attach Form 8889	25	
26	Moving expenses. Attach Form 3903	26	
27	Deductible part of self-employment tax. Attach Schedule SE	27	911.
28	Self-employed SEP, SIMPLE, and qualified plans	28	
29	Self-employed health insurance deduction	29	
30	Penalty on early withdrawal of savings	30	
31a	Alimony paid b Recipient's SSN ▶	31a	
32	IRA deduction	32	
33	Student loan interest deduction	33	
34	Tuition and fees. Attach Form 8917	34	
35	Domestic production activities deduction. Attach Form 8903	35	
36	Add lines 23 through 35	36	911.
37	Subtract line 36 from line 22. This is your **adjusted gross income** ▶	37	103,345.

For Disclosure, Privacy Act, and Paperwork Reduction Act Notice, see separate instructions.
BCA
Form **1040** (2015)

Chapter 4-2 Page 1

Harak Gala, CPA

Form 1040 (2015) Mark & Mary Taxpayer   400-02-1005   Page **2**

Tax and Credits	38 Amount from line 37 (adjusted gross income)	38	109,345.
Standard Deduction for—	39a Check: ☐ You were born before Jan. 2, 1951, ☐ Blind. ☐ Spouse was born before Jan. 2, 1951, ☐ Blind. Total boxes checked ▶ 39a		
• People who check any box on line 39a or 39b or who can be claimed as a dependent, see instructions.	b If your spouse itemizes on a separate return or you were a dual-status alien, check here ▶ 39b		
	40 Itemized deductions (from Schedule A) or your standard deduction (see left margin)	40	22,300.
	41 Subtract line 40 from line 38	41	87,045.
	42 Exemptions. If line 38 is $154,950 or less, multiply $4,000 by the number on line 6d. Otherwise, see instructions	42	8,000.
• All others:	43 Taxable income. Subtract line 42 from line 41. If line 42 is more than line 41, enter -0-	43	79,045.
Single or Married filing separately, $6,300	44 Tax (see instructions). Check if any from: a ☐ Form(s) 8814 b ☐ Form 4972 c ☐	44	11,064.
Married filing jointly or Qualifying widow(er), $12,600	45 Alternative minimum tax (see instructions). Attach Form 6251	45	
	46 Excess advance premium tax credit repayment. Attach Form 8962	46	
Head of household, $9,250	47 Add lines 44, 45, and 46 ▶	47	11,064.
	48 Foreign tax credit. Attach Form 1116 if required	48	
	49 Credit for child and dependent care expenses. Attach Form 2441	49	
	50 Education credits from Form 8863, line 19	50	
	51 Retirement savings contributions credit. Attach Form 8880	51	
	52 Child tax credit. Attach Schedule 8812, if required	52	
	53 Residential energy credits. Attach Form 5695	53	
	54 Other credits from Form: a ☐ 3800 b ☐ 8801 c ☐	54	
	55 Add lines 48 through 54. These are your total credits	55	
	56 Subtract line 55 from line 47. If line 55 is more than line 47, enter -0- ▶	56	11,064.
	57 Self-employment tax. Attach Schedule SE	57	1,922.
Other Taxes	58 Unreported social security and Medicare tax from Form: a ☐ 4137 b ☐ 8919	58	
	59 Additional tax on IRAs, other qualified retirement plans, etc. Attach Form 5329 if required	59	
	60a Household employment taxes from Schedule H	60a	
	b First-time homebuyer credit repayment. Attach Form 5405 if required	60b	
	61 Health care: individual responsibility (see instructions) Full-year coverage ☒	61	
	62 Taxes from: a ☐ Form 8959 b ☐ Form 8960 c ☐ instructions; enter code(s)	62	
	63 Add lines 56 through 62. This is your total tax ▶	63	12,986. After
Payments	64 Federal income tax withheld from Forms W-2 and 1099	64	18,000.
If you have a qualifying child, attach Schedule EIC.	65 2015 estimated tax payments and amount applied from 2014 return	65	
	66a Earned income credit (EIC)	66a	
	b Nontaxable combat pay election 66b		
	67 Additional child tax credit. Attach Form 8812	67	
	68 American opportunity credit from Form 8863, line 8	68	
	69 Net premium tax credit. Attach Form 8962	69	
	70 Amount paid with request for extension to file	70	
	71 Excess social security and tier 1 RRTA tax withheld	71	
	72 Credit for federal tax on fuels. Attach Form 4136	72	
	73 Credits from Form: a ☐ 2439 b ☐ Reserved c ☐ 8885 d ☐	73	
	74 Add lines 64, 65, 66a, and 67 through 73. These are your total payments ▶	74	18,000.
Refund	75 If line 74 is more than line 63, subtract line 63 from line 74. This is the amount you overpaid	75	5,114.
	76a Amount of line 75 you want refunded to you. If Form 8888 is attached, check here ▶ ☐	76a	5,114.
Direct deposit? See instructions.	▶ b Routing number		
	▶ c Type: ☐ Checking ☐ Savings		
	▶ d Account number		
	77 Amount of line 75 you want applied to your 2016 estimated tax ▶ 77		
Amount You Owe	78 Amount you owe. Subtract line 74 from line 63. For details on how to pay, see instructions ▶	78	
	79 Estimated tax penalty (see instructions) 79		
Third Party Designee	Do you want to allow another person to discuss this return with the IRS (see instructions)? ☒ Yes. Complete below. ☐ No		
	Designee's name ▶ Harak Gala CPA Phone no. ▶ 301-912-3450 Personal identification number (PIN) ▶ 87941		
Sign Here	Under penalties of perjury, I declare that I have examined this return and accompanying schedules and statements, and to the best of my knowledge and belief, they are true, correct, and complete. Declaration of preparer (other than taxpayer) is based on all information of which preparer has any knowledge.		
Joint return? See instructions. Keep a copy for your records.	Your signature Date Your occupation: Construction Manager Daytime phone number		
	Spouse's signature. If a joint return, both must sign. Date Spouse's occupation: Self Employed If the IRS sent you an Identity Protection PIN, enter it here (see inst.)		
Paid Preparer Use Only	Print/Type preparer's name: Harak Gala CPA Preparer's signature: Harak Gala CPA Date: 10/23/2016 Check ☐ if self-employed PTIN: P01201436		
	Firm's name ▶ eTax Corporation Firm's EIN ▶ 57-1912619		
	Firm's address ▶ 727 Thornwood Dr, GORNTON MD 21113 Phone no. 301-912-3450		

Form **1040** (2015)

Cut Your Tax In Half

SCHEDULE E (Form 1040)
Department of the Treasury
Internal Revenue Service (99)

Supplemental Income and Loss
(From rental real estate, royalties, partnerships, S corporations, estates, trusts, REMICs, etc.)
► Attach to Form 1040, 1040NR, or Form 1041.
► Information about Schedule E and its separate instructions is at www.irs.gov/schedulee.

OMB No. 1545-0074
2015
Attachment Sequence No. **13**

Name(s) shown on return: Mark & Mary Taxpayer
Your social security no.: 400-02-1005

Part I — Income or Loss From Rental Real Estate and Royalties
Note: If you are in the business of renting personal property, use Schedule C or C-EZ (see instructions). If you are an individual, report farm rental income or loss from **Form 4835** on page 2, line 40.

A Did you make any payments in 2015 that would require you to file Form(s) 1099? ☐ Yes ☒ No
B If "Yes," did you or will you file all required Forms 1099? ☐ Yes ☐ No

1a Physical address of each property (street, city, state, Zip code)
A 123 Rental Way
B 456 Rental Street
C

1b	Type of Property (from list below)	2 For each rental real estate property listed above, report the number of fair rental and personal use days. Check the QJV box only if you meet the requirements to file as a qualified joint venture. See instructions.		Fair Rental Days	Personal Use Days	QJV
A	2		A	365		
B	2		B	365		
C			C			

Type of Property:
1 Single Family Residence   3 Vacation/Short-Term Rental   5 Land   7 Self-Rental
2 Multi-Family Residence   4 Commercial   6 Royalties   8 Other (describe)

Income:	Properties:		A	B	C
3 Rents received		3	15,000.	19,000.	
4 Royalties received		4			
Expenses:					
5 Advertising		5			
6 Auto and travel (see instructions)		6	140.	280.	
7 Cleaning and maintenance		7	500.	750.	
8 Commissions		8			
9 Insurance		9	780.	840.	
10 Legal and other professional fees		10			
11 Management fees		11			
12 Mortgage interest paid to banks, etc. (see instructions)		12	15,500.	18,000.	
13 Other interest		13			
14 Repairs		14	2,980.	3,750.	
15 Supplies		15			
16 Taxes		16	4,000.	5,000.	
17 Utilities		17			
18 Depreciation expense or depletion		18	13,457.	13,817.	
19 Other (list) ►		19			
20 Total expenses. Add lines 5 through 19		20	37,357.	42,437.	
21 Subtract line 20 from line 3 (rents) and/or 4 (royalties). If result is a (loss), see instructions to find out if you must file **Form 6198**		21	(22,357.)	(24,437.)	
22 Deductible rental real estate loss after limitation, if any, on **Form 8582** (see instructions)		22	22,357.)(	24,437.)(	
23a Total of all amounts reported on line 3 for all rental properties		23a	33,000.		
b Total of all amounts reported on line 4 for all royalty properties		23b			
c Total of all amounts reported on line 12 for all properties		23c	33,500.		
d Total of all amounts reported on line 18 for all properties		23d	27,274.		
e Total of all amounts reported on line 20 for all properties		23e	79,794.		
24 **Income**. Add positive amounts shown on line 21. Do not include any losses		24			
25 **Losses**. Add royalty losses from line 21 and rental real estate losses from line 22. Enter total losses here		25)(	46,794.)(		
26 **Total rental real estate and royalty income or (loss)**. Combine lines 24 and 25. Enter the result here. If Parts II, III, IV, and line 40 on page 2 do not apply to you, also enter this amount on Form 1040, line 17, or Form 1040NR, line 18. Otherwise, include this amount in the total on line 41 on page 2		26	(46,794.)		

For Paperwork Reduction Act Notice, see the separate instructions.   Schedule E (Form 1040) 2015

BCA
Chapter 4-2 Page 3

Notes

Notes

CHAPTER 5

Social-Security Taxes

• • •

Ronald and Jennifer were enjoying their new retirement. After talking to the couple for several minutes, I learned the following about them:

1. They did not want to pay any taxes, if possible.
2. They did not like losing money.
3. They wanted to make sure they would have enough money during their lifetime.

I looked at their investment statements and saw they had saved a sizable amount of money, most of which was in tax-free investments.

As per the copy of their tax return, their income was as follows:

1. $4,000 in taxable interest
2. $47,000 in tax-free interest
3. $905 in taxable dividends
4. $1,800 in capital gain
5. $10,000 in Ronald's pension
6. $1,800 in capital gains
7. $31,000 from Ronald's social security
8. $29,000 from Jennifer's social security

This added up to a total income of $92,705 and a total tax liability of $5,014 in federal taxes in 2014. Figure 5-1 shows a copy of their tax return.

Author: Congratulations, Ronald and Jennifer. You have saved very well for your retirement.

Ronald: Yes, we worked very hard during our working years and paid a lot of taxes. We want to make sure we do not pay a single penny more in taxes than is absolutely necessary.

Author: I don't blame you. It's your right to minimize your taxes through tax planning.

Ronald: That's why we invested the bulk of our money in tax-free investments: I like the term "tax-free." Ideally, we don't want to pay any taxes at this stage of our life and wish the rest of our income also would be tax-free. You helped our daughter, Rhonda and son-in-law Ray, with their taxes. Can you help us with reducing our taxes too? After all, when we contributed to Social Security, we never got the tax deduction. Now we are just getting our money back—why do we have to pay taxes on our own money?

Author: I can certainly understand your frustration. Let's review your tax return. It looks like you paid $5,014 in federal taxes for 2015.

Ronald: That's correct. It would have been more if we didn't have tax-free investments.

Author: Believe it or not, it's your tax-free investments that are actually causing you to pay more taxes.

Ronald: I don't understand that! How can a tax-free investment make us pay more taxes?

Author: Let me show you your 2015 tax return prepared in another way. [Readers can view this in figure 5-2.] At this time, I am not suggesting changing any of your investments, so they all stay the way they are, except for the tax-free ones. We would make changes only after suitability and risk-tolerance analysis, and the changes must be in your best interest. But for argument's sake, suppose we replace all your tax-free municipal-bond investments with tax-deferred investments. All your taxes will go away. You would have paid $0 in taxes.

Ronald: What? How can that be?

Author: Certain types of income can make more of your social-security income taxable. Income from the tax-free muni bonds is not taxable for federal purposes, but it does get added to your income while calculating the taxability of the social-security income. On the other hand, tax-deferred investments do not get added to the social-security income when we calculate its taxability.

Ronald: Wow! I did not know that. Should we change our investments?

Author: I don't know yet. We need to meet again. After asking you more questions and performing a suitability analysis, I will help you decide whether making changes in your investments is in your best interest.

Ronald: Sounds interesting. We definitely would like to learn more.

Cut Your Tax In Half

Form 1040 U.S. Individual Income Tax Return 2015

Name: Ronald Retiree
Spouse: Jennifer Retiree
Address: 123 Retirement Road, COLUMBIA MD 21045
SSN: 400-01-1006
Spouse SSN: 400-01-2006

Filing Status: Married filing jointly

Exemptions: Yourself, Spouse — Total: 2

Income

7	Wages, salaries, tips, etc.	
8a	Taxable interest	4,000
8b	Tax-exempt interest	47,000
9a	Ordinary dividends	905
9b	Qualified dividends	500
13	Capital gain or (loss)	1,800
16a	Pensions and annuities	1,000
16b	Taxable amount	10,000
20a	Social security benefits	60,000
20b	Taxable amount	48,249
22	**Total income**	64,954

Adjusted Gross Income

37	Adjusted gross income	64,954

Figure 5-1 Page 1

59

Harak Gala, CPA

Figure 5-1 Page 2

Cut Your Tax In Half

Form 1040 — U.S. Individual Income Tax Return (2015)

Your first name and initial: Ronald Retirees
Your social security number: 400-02-1006
Spouse's first name and initial: Jennifer Retirees
Spouse's social security number: 400-01-2006
Home address: 123 Retirement Road
City, town or post office, state, and ZIP code: COLUMBIA MD 21045-

Filing Status: 2 — Married filing jointly (even if only one had income)

Exemptions:
- 6a [X] Yourself
- 6b [X] Spouse
- Boxes checked on 6a and 6b: 2
- Total number of exemptions claimed: 2

Income

7	Wages, salaries, tips, etc. Attach Form(s) W-2	
8a	Taxable interest	4,000.
8b	Tax-exempt interest	
9a	Ordinary dividends	905.
9b	Qualified dividends	500.
10	Taxable refunds, credits, or offsets of state and local income taxes	
11	Alimony received	
12	Business income or (loss)	
13	Capital gain or (loss)	1,860.
14	Other gains or (losses)	
15a	IRA distributions	
15b	Taxable amount	
16a	Pensions and annuities — 1,000.	
16b	Taxable amount	10,000.
17	Rental real estate, royalties, partnerships, S corporations, trusts, etc.	
18	Farm income or (loss)	
19	Unemployment compensation	
20a	Social security benefits — 60,000.	
20b	Taxable amount	8,299.
21	Other income	
22	**Total income**	25,064.

Adjusted Gross Income

23	Educator expenses	
24	Certain business expenses of reservists, performing artists, and fee-basis gov. officials	
25	Health savings account deduction	
26	Moving expenses	
27	Deductible part of self-employment tax	
28	Self-employed SEP, SIMPLE, and qualified plans	
29	Self-employed health insurance deduction	
30	Penalty on early withdrawal of savings	
31a	Alimony paid	
32	IRA deduction	
33	Student loan interest deduction	
34	Tuition and fees	
35	Domestic production activities deduction	
36	Add lines 23 through 35	
37	**Adjusted gross income**	25,064.

Figure 5-2 Page 1

Harak Gala, CPA

Figure 5-2 Page 2

CHAPTER 6

Small-Business Retirement Plans

• • •

As a small-business owner, you have worked very hard to build a successful business. Now it is time to decide how to build and accumulate wealth in the most tax-efficient way. Small-business retirement plans can help you save for the future and at the same time offer many tax advantages. There are two primary categories of small-business retirement plans: defined-contribution (DC) plans and defined-benefit (DB) plans. The purpose of this chapter is not to make you an expert in these plans; instead, the goal is simply to point out that many different kinds of plans are available that could have a large impact on taxes. DB plans are more complex and should *not* be established without the help of professionals.

Defined-Contribution Plans (DC):

With DC plans, the annual contributions to the plan are defined. Both employers and employees can contribute to such plans. Employers' contributions are generally based on a predetermined formula, which is usually some percentage of the employee's salary. Each eligible employee can determine his or her own contribution, subject to some limits. A DC plan provides each participant a separate account. It does not guarantee any specific amount of benefits at retirement. Examples of defined-contribution plans include these: 401(k), 403(b), 457, individual 401(k), Simplified Employee Pension (SEP) plan, SIMPLE IRA, profit-sharing plan, and ESOP. Different DC plans have different contribution limits, and formulas to calculate the maximum contribution vary from plan to plan. The maximum annual contribution in some of these plans is $53,000, while others have much lower maximum annual contributions. Depending on your situation, some plans will suit you better than others.

DEFINED-BENEFIT PLANS (DB):

A DB plan guarantees a certain amount of benefit to each participant at retirement. It is typically funded by employer contributions and is subject to some limits. (Current contribution is calculated *based on* those benefit limits.) DB plans could be traditional DB plans or 419(e) plans. In either one, the plan assets typically are held in a trust account. The amount of maximum benefit allowed in 2017 was $215,000 or 100 percent of pay, whichever is less. Calculations of annual contributions are very complex and do require help from a specialist. DB plans are for financially stable businesses only, as employers must have ongoing financial stability to fund such plans.

Traditional Defined-Benefit Plans: It is possible to use many different kinds of investments to fund these plans.

419(e) fully insured plans—formerly known as 412(i) plans: As these plans are fully insured, they have to be funded by insurance products only. Typically, the funding vehicles are annuity products. Life-insurance products can be added to the plan, subject to certain limitations. Of all the small-business retirement plans, 419(e) plans can have the highest initial contribution, resulting in the highest possible tax deduction. Over the years, some people have tried to abuse these plans, which resulted in bad press. The IRS stepped in and issued guidance intended to curb perceived abuses.

Cash-Balance Plans (Hybrid Plan): The cash-balance plan is usually referred to as a hybrid plan, because it combines features of both DB and DC plans. It has become very popular in recent years, as it not only has a specified amount of benefit at retirement like a DB plan but also has individual separate accounts like DC plans.

DC plans can be combined with DB plans with some limitations. DB plans are more age-dependent than are DC plans. Let us look at the different retirement plans based on participant age. At a younger age, DC plans allow more contributions. At an older age, DB plans usually allow more contributions. The following chart shows the maximum allowable contribution based on a salary of $265,000. The amounts do not increase if the salary grows beyond $265,000 ($270,000 in 2017); however, the amounts can go down if the salary decreases.

Figures 6-1 to 6-4 show the maximum contributions for different plans based on W-2 income and participant age. Let us look at figure 6-1. In the chart, maximum contributions allowed for individual 401(k) and SEP are the same $53,000 for a forty-year-old person, but both could be drastically different at a lower salary. Without thorough knowledge of the plans, it is easy to make the wrong choice(s). A good plan for one business may not be good for another. Let's look at some real-life situations.

John and Jessica are both fifty years old. Both of them are doctors in a private medical practice. Their business entity is an S corporation. Each of them takes $265,000 salary, and the corporation issues a W-2 to each of them at the end of the year. They have $888,000 worth of nonqualified investments. Their combined federal and state-tax bracket is 46 percent. Each of them is eligible for $205,000 contribution in the defined-benefit plan. If they do decide to contribute a total of $410,000 ($205,000 each) in a defined-benefit plan, they can save $188,000 in taxes. They need to come up with an additional $222,000—we get this by subtracting the $188,000 saved in taxes from the $410,000 maximum contribution—to fund the plan. They can do this by repositioning 25 percent of their nonqualified funds from their individual names to the DB plan; however, a professional financial adviser should complete a thorough suitability analysis to ensure any change in investments would be in John and Jessica's best interest.

Once they retire, they will need to talk to a financial adviser about the possibility of rolling the DB plan funds over into their IRA. A financial adviser has to make sure that rolling over to an IRA is their best option. If they *do* decide to roll over to an IRA, they can make another ten-year plan of converting this IRA into a Roth IRA. They should do this with the help of a CPA in the most tax-efficient way. CPAs and financial advisers working together can also design John and Jessica's social-security strategy. With proper tax and financial planning, most of their retirement income can be tax-free by the time they reach seventy, and they won't have to worry about required minimum distributions (RMD).

Without a proper plan, their investments would have remained taxable forever. With proper planning, however, John and Jessica can convert their taxable investments into tax-deferred investments today, and they will be able to move from tax-deferred investments to tax-free investments in the future.

Maximum Deductible Contribution for a 40 Years Old Individual in 2015

W-2 Income	SEP IRA	Individual 401(k)	Traditional DB Plan Only (Approximately)	Traditional DB Plan plus 401(k) (Approximately)
$100,000	$25,000	$43,000	$35,000	$59,000
$150,000	$37,500	$53,000	$53,000	$80,000
$200,000	$50,000	$53,000	$71,000	$101,000
$250,000	$53,000	$53,000	$83,000	$116,000
$265,000	$53,000	$53,000	$87,000	$120,900

Figure 6-1

**Maximum Deductible Contribution for a
45 Years Old Individual in 2015**

W-2 Income	SEP IRA	Individual 401(k)	Traditional DB Plan Only (Approximately)	Traditional DB Plan plus 401(k) (Approximately)
$100,000	$25,000	$43,000	$55,000	$79,000
$150,000	$37,500	$53,000	$82,000	$109,000
$200,000	$50,000	$53,000	$110,000	$140,000
$250,000	$53,000	$53,000	$128,000	$161,000
$265,000	$53,000	$53,000	$135,000	$168,900

Figure 6-2

**Maximum Deductible Contribution for a
50 Years Old Individual in 2015**

W-2 Income	SEP IRA	Individual 401(k)	Traditional DB Plan Only (Approximately)	Traditional DB Plan plus 401(k) (Approximately)
$100,000	$25,000	$43,000	$67,000	$97,000
$150,000	$37,500	$53,000	$100,000	$133,000
$200,000	$50,000	$53,000	$134,000	$170,000
$250,000	$53,000	$53,000	$156,000	$195,000
$265,000	$53,000	$53,000	$166,000	$205,900

Figure 6-3

**Maximum Deductible Contribution for a
55 Years Old Individual in 2015**

W-2 Income	SEP IRA	Individual 401(k)	Traditional DB Plan Only (Approximately)	Traditional DB Plan plus 401(k) (Approximately)
$100,000	$25,000	$43,000	$82,000	$112,000
$150,000	$37,500	$53,000	$123,000	$156,000
$200,000	$50,000	$53,000	$164,000	$200,000
$250,000	$53,000	$53,000	$191,000	$230,000
$265,000	$53,000	$53,000	$202,000	$241,900

Figure 6-4

Notes

Notes

CHAPTER 7

Tax-Free Retirement Using IRS Notice 2014-54

• • •

IN THE LAST CHAPTER, we covered the tax-planning advantages of using small-business retirement plans. But what if you don't own a business? What if you work as a W-2 employee, make good money, and want to invest more in your retirement plan? Your 401(k) would have allowed a maximum of $18,000 a year—$24,000 if you are fifty years or older—in 2016. You may want to contribute more than that but find you aren't eligible for IRA or Roth IRA contributions because you make too much money.

If business owners can contribute six-figure amounts to their retirement plans, why can't you? You are no less professional. Until recently, this was a real problem—but everything changed overnight on September 18, 2014.

The 401(k) or 403(b) plans of some companies allow employees to make additional contributions beyond allowable limits. (Again, allowable limits are $18,000 for those under fifty and $24,000 for those fifty and older.) If your company does, you were allowed annual contributions of as much as $54,000 in 2017. Any contributions beyond the limits of $18,000 or $24,000 are considered nondeductible contributions. You can have a combination of a Roth 401(k) and a deductible traditional 401(k), but the total contribution to both cannot exceed the allowable limits of $18,000 or $24,000. After you reach these limits, the rest of the contribution is designated as nondeductible 401(k).

Until now, converting this nondeductible 401(k) contribution into Roth was confusing and not tax-efficient, but it became much easier with the release of IRS Notice 2014-54 in September 2014. Now, high-income earners can contribute up to $54,000 to their 401(k) plans annually, *if* the plan documents allow it. Part of this contribution goes to either a "pretax" 401(k) plan or Roth 401(k), and the rest goes to a nondeductible 401(k) plan. When the employee retires or changes job, he or she can roll over the entire amount. "Pretax" money gets rolled over to a traditional IRA and considered nontaxable funds; Roth 401(k) funds get rolled over to a Roth IRA without any taxes or penalties. Of course, before you do any rollovers, you need to consult your financial adviser to make sure this is the best strategy for *you*.

We discussed the backdoor Roth IRA in chapter 1. That is a great strategy if you are just starting out and do not have any IRA accounts. If you *do* have significant money in an IRA, the backdoor Roth IRA won't work; however, if your company allows nondeductible 401(k) contributions, you have a potential for tax-free conversion of a nondeductible 401(k) into a Roth IRA. Those who want to contribute more can now contribute up to the maximum allowable after-tax contributions. Their goal should be to roll over into a Roth IRA at termination of employment. Any money available in a traditional 401(k) should be rolled over to a traditional IRA at the same time.

For 2017, the total retirement contribution could not exceed $54,000. This total consists of all the money going into the plan, including employer match or discretionary contributions. Top-heavy rules and other nondiscriminatory tests may reduce the allowable limit of $54,000. Based on employee participation, the plan administrator can determine the amount of maximum after-tax contributions allowed. If your retirement account contains your company stock, you will have to take into account the Net Unrealized Appreciation (NUA) rules before you make a decision to roll funds over. (If you want to know more about NUA, please contact me through our company website http://www.etaxonline.com. I will be glad to send it to you electronically.)

Notes

Notes

CHAPTER 8

Tax-Free Retirement Using IRS Code Sections 7702 & 72(e)

• • •

IN THE LAST CHAPTER, we discussed creating tax-free retirement if your company retirement plan allows nondeductible contributions…but what if your company plan does *not* allow nondeductible contributions? If you don't own a business, you can't create your own retirement plan, but you may not be allowed to contribute to a Roth IRA or a deductible IRA because your income is too high. Maybe you maxed out your normal 401(k) but want to contribute more for your retirement in the tax-advantaged way. What do you do?

Now imagine your spouse's situation is even worse. His or her company does not offer any kind of retirement plan. Your spouse contributes $5,500 to a Roth IRA, but that is not enough for your goals. Are you out of luck? *No.* There is a solution in using IRS codes 7702 and 72(e) for life insurance. You might think life insurance is only for protecting the family in case of the primary breadwinner's premature death and wonder what it has to do with tax-free retirement. Yes, it's true that the primary purpose of life insurance is the death benefit, but innovations by life-insurance companies—combined with the IRS codes—have created many living benefits. In this chapter, I am talking about a life-insurance product called Indexed Universal Life (IUL).

A properly structured IUL can provide the following advantages:

1. Income tax–free death benefits for the beneficiaries
2. May help reduce or eliminate estate taxes

3. Income tax–deferred growth of cash values
4. Income tax–free income through policy loans, creating tax-free retirement-income potential.
5. No IRS total-contribution limits, though to get better tax advantages, it may be necessary to divide the total contribution over four to seven years, instead of paying over a single premium
6. No IRS penalties on distributions before age fifty-nine and a half
7. Flexibility of premium payments
8. If the premium is missed in one year, you can make it up in the following years
9. No restrictions on ownership
10. Potential for tax-free benefits for long-term care
11. Potential for tax-free benefits for chronic illness
12. Can be used as a college-funding vehicle
13. Can be used for business-planning solutions

No other single product can provide all these benefits. It sounds too good to be true, doesn't it? Usually, when people think about life insurance, they consider it an expense. They want to buy the maximum amount of death benefit with as little premium as possible. Many people consider life insurance a necessary evil—the benefits after your death are not too exciting.

But suppose I tell you the minimum monthly premium for the amount of death benefit you are considering will be $300. What would your reaction be? You might say it's too expensive. You might also ask me whether it can be made cheaper. Am I right? Now, if I suggest that, instead of paying $300, you pay $1,500 per month for the same death benefit, how would you react?

You might think I am making fun of you. You might laugh it off. But I'm serious. Some rich people back in the 1970s were putting hundreds of thousands of dollars in insurance premiums for a relatively small benefit. Why? What did they know that most people did not? Rich people back then knew the power of the living benefits of life insurance. They were able to turn hundreds of thousands of dollars into millions of dollars without paying any taxes. The government caught on over time and made some changes in the IRS code section 7702, which puts some restrictions on how much, over what period, and when you can put money into life insurance to take advantage of all the tax benefits it offers. If you put in too much money too fast, they consider the life-insurance policy a modified-endowment contract (MEC), and the tax benefits will be reduced.

In order to take all the tax advantages life insurance offers, the policy must be non-MEC, as described in code section 7702. Based on your age, the total premium you put into the life-insurance policy should be spread at least over a four- to seven-year period to make the policy non-MEC as specified in the IRS code. Therefore, the maximum amount you can contribute in a given year is determined by the IRS. With IRAs and 401(k)s, if you miss the contribution one year, you cannot make it up in subsequent years. With life insurance, however, if you miss a payment one year, you can make it up in the following years. The minimum payment is determined by the insurance company to cover the cost of the insurance and administrative expenses.

In the beginning of this chapter, we listed many potential benefits of life insurance. Although the primary purpose of the insurance is to serve as a death benefit, the tax benefits are also important. You may well consider it as part of your total investment portfolio.

Notes

Notes

CHAPTER 9

Working as a Team

• • •

IN THE PREVIOUS CHAPTERS, I gave you a few examples how you can reduce your taxes. These scenarios may or may not apply to you. Don't worry, if your situation is completely different. There are many more strategies available that I have not mentioned in this book. Some of these include the following:

- Health care–related expenses
- Family limited partnerships
- Gifting of income-producing assets to family members
- Donating appreciable stocks to charity
- Family trusts
- Charitable lead trusts
- Charitable remainder trusts
- Sale and leaseback arrangements
- Combining passive losses with passive income
- Oil and gas investments
- Properly registered tax shelters

The list is endless. The purpose of this book is not to describe all these strategies in detail and make you an expert in taxes. It is to emphasize the importance of planning ahead. Although the strategies described in this book can be applied to many different income groups, they can be used more effectively by high-income professionals.

High-income professionals carry most of the tax burden in the current tax environment. They not only pay the regular income tax for both the federal and state levels but also could be subjected to Alternate Minimum Tax (AMT), Net Investment Income Tax (NIT), new Medicare taxes, and much more. They also lose many of the available deductions and credits. As a matter of fact, many times, high-income professionals pay a higher percentage of taxes compared to super wealthy people. Why? Because many times they are so busy with their professional work that they don't have time for preplanning—and it's too late when they go to their tax preparer in March or April to finish their tax returns. Very rich people, on the other hand, have access to their advisers throughout the year. Some advisers even work for them as employees.

There is no reason high-income professionals can't have access to the proper advice, similar to their super-rich counterparts. If they can bring their tax advisers and financial advisers under one roof, they also can have access to great advice specially tailored to their needs. Unfortunately, this is not true for most of you. Your CPA wants to do the best for you but he or she may not have all the information about your assets or finances. He or she may not have expertise in dealing with your financial goals and objectives. Your financial advisor wants to do the best for you but his or her tax knowledge may be limited and his or her plan may make you pay more taxes than necessary. If they prepare a plan for you without talking to each other, there could be a conflict in those plans. It is very important that they talk to each other, remove those conflicts, and work together in your best interest.

Many CPAs don't like referring their clients to other professionals. I can certainly understand why: they don't want their clients to get hurt by other unknown professionals. I have gone through that situation myself, when I referred a tax client to one mortgage broker. To avoid this risk, it is necessary for a CPA to create an ongoing relationship with a financial adviser—this way, the CPA is not dealing with a stranger.

Similarly, I have too often seen tax inefficiencies in my tax clients' investments at the hands of their financial advisers. This was the ultimate reason I became a financial adviser myself. I urge financial advisers to act proactively to form alliances with CPAs for their clients' benefit.

New technologies are changing how we work at a very fast rate. It is not difficult for different professionals to work together for your benefit. Everybody needs to connect and collaborate. Professionals need to make their thoughts and choices known to others, for increased success for everyone.

I hope this book helps in creating a different kind of mind-set when it comes to tax and financial planning. You are now in a better position to demand what you want, need, and deserve from your professionals.

I have given a few ways to reduce your taxes by working with your financial adviser and CPA. Again, however, I must reiterate that you should not implement any of these strategies yourself. Tax laws are never straightforward. There are exceptions, and there are exceptions to the exceptions—and there are exceptions to the exceptions to the exceptions. What works for one person may not work for you. My hope is that this book has prepared you to ask more questions of the professionals you are working with and that doing so results in a better outcome for you.

Notes

Notes

AUTHOR'S NOTE

• • •

THIS BOOK IS JUST A starting point. The tax laws are constantly changing. In all likelihood, big changes will be coming in 2017. This may lead to even more tax-planning opportunities. Start your own tax reduction planning process by visiting http://www.CutYourTaxInHalf.com

Also sign up for our monthly newsletters and ongoing alerts. Please visit our website, http://www.etaxonline.com, to sign up.

The website contains many different articles, videos, illustrations, calculators, and presentations on topics such as the following:

- Business planning
- College planning
- Estate planning
- Financial planning
- Protection planning
- Retirement planning
- Social-security planning
- Tax planning

The website also contains articles on special life situations. Please feel free to download these for your own reference and use, but remember this information is for educational purposes only. You will still need help from professionals to implement any of the suggestions made in those articles.

**START YOUR OWN
TAX REDUCTION
PLANNING PROCESS**
visit
http://www.CutYourTaxInHalf.com

www.ingramcontent.com/pod-product-compliance
Lightning Source LLC
Chambersburg PA
CBHW070049210526
45170CB00012B/631